Growing Up With Jesus

devotions for preschoolers

REVIEW AND HERALD® PUBLISHING ASSOCIATION
HAGERSTOWN, MD 21740

Copyright © 1993 by
Review and Herald® Publishing Association

The authors assume full responsibility for the accuracy of all facts and quotations as cited in this book.

This book was
Edited by Richard W. Coffen and Raymond H. Woolsey
Designed by Bill Kirstein
Cover art by Patricia Wegh
Photos by Joel Springer
Typeset: Goudy Old Style

PRINTED IN U.S.A.

98 97 96 95 94 93   10 9 8 7 6 5 4 3 2 1

R&H Cataloging Service
 Growing up with Jesus.

 1. Children—Religious life. 2. Devotional
literature—Juvenile. 3. Devotional calendars—
Seventh-day Adventist.
                242.62

ISBN 0-8280-0780-2

Contributing Authors

Amelia Christian Baker was born in New Orleans, Louisiana, but has also lived in California and now Arkansas. Amelia studied religion and sociology at California State College and also attended Loma Linda University and later Arkansas Tech University. Mrs. Baker has six children and currently operates a small publishing business in Little Rock. She is also a credentialed Bible instructor. Other responsibilities she has held include radio news reporter, youth counselor, college instructor, and librarian.

Faith Johnson Crumbly's professional roles have included speechwriter and ghostwriter for business executives, editor and writer for business and community newsletters, and writer for community newspapers. But for many more years her "heart-writing" has produced plays, poetry, songs, speeches, and programs for the children in her home, home churches, and church and public schools. She has been published in such magazines as *Insight*, *Kids' Stuff*, *Lake Union Herald*, and *Cornerstone Connections*. Faith says that her favorite audience and the heroes in much of her writing are her husband, Edward, and their five children.

Mary H. Duplex has authored three children's books and has had numerous short stories published in *Guide*, *Primary Treasure*, and *Our Little Friend*. She has four grown children and 15 grandchildren. Mary lives in Washington State with her husband, Sid, and their miniature schnauzer named Schultzie.

Crystal B. Earnhardt is a freelance author and has had two books published—*Annie's Secret* and *Will You Still Love Me Tomorrow?* Her byline has also appeared in such periodicals as *Guide*, *Insight*, *Cornerstone Connections*, and *Our Little Friend*. She has two children, and her husband is currently an evangelist employed by Amazing Facts.

Cheryl Woolsey Holloway has a B.S. in early childhood and elementary education and an M.A. in education, neither of which was full preparation for her role as mother of four children! Cheryl has taught church school in Indonesia and home school in Michigan. She and her husband, David, and their children live on the Blackfeet Indian reservation beside Glacier National Park. Currently she is in charge of the Early Childhood Education Department at the Blackfeet Community College. She has written numerous materials for children and young adults, as well as two books, *Time Out for Moms* and *Creative Devotions*.

Pat Humphrey is former editor of *Kids' Stuff* magazine. Currently she is a freelance writer and editor. She currently provides home

3

schooling for her two children, Brandon, age 9, and Candice, age 12. Pat loves working with children and telling stories.

A former grade school teacher, **Virginia L. Kroll** has been writing for only eight years. During that short time she has had an incredible 1,600 articles/stories accepted by juvenile magazines, as well as 14 picture books. She is currently a full-time writer-lecturer and mother of six children.

Though a librarian and teacher by profession, **Eileen E. Lantry**'s first love is nature. She enjoys studying nature, collecting from " 'God's second book,' and teaching in all its forms." Her three sons, two grandsons, and students from kindergarten to college have benefited from this interest.

The Lantrys spent 14 years as missionaries in the Far East, mostly in Singapore and Sabah. Eileen enjoys giving Bible studies, hiking, camping, and cross-country skiing. She has published 13 books and many stories and articles, but she says that the most important thing in her life is that she loves Jesus.

Patty Mostert Marsh of Centralia, Missouri, spends quality time with her husband, Larry, and their two teenage daughters. She also makes time for writing amid her responsibilities as a teacher at Sunnydale Academy and busy vocalist-pianist. Her magazine articles have been published in *Celebration* and *Mid-America Adventist Outlook*.

Patty encourages young mothers to "cherish the time you spend with your children. You will never regret it."

Mary Meade Montaque is a public school elementary principal in Massachusetts. Prior to that she has worked as a curriculum specialist, a science teacher at Greateer New York Academy, assistant professor for experiential education, chemistry instructor, and the developer-director for the Career Life Planning Center at Atlantic Union College. In her leisure Mary enjoys camping, reading, bird watching, traveling, sewing, and gardening. She has two young children.

Edwina Ruth Grice Neely combines the practical experience of raising four children with 10 years in the field of speech pathology (she holds a master's degree in speech pathology and audiology from the University of Houston) and 10 years in the field of child care services and children's ministries. She founded and directs Loving Angel's Daycare: The Quality Christian Learning Place. She is also a pastor's wife and currently serves as family ministries director and Vacation Bible School director at the Takoma Park Seventh-day Adventist Church. Edwina holds seminars on creative learning techniques for preschoolers, effective communication, and family worship.

Karen Nicola is a full-time homemaker, and has taught in the children's Sabbath school divisions for 13 years in her local church. Karen and her husband, Steve, and their daughter, Joanna, live in the foothills of northern California. As of the time of writing, they were waiting to travel to Moscow to bring home their adopted son.

Nina Coombs Pykare, of Warren, Ohio, has been writing ever since she could hold a pencil, and her first work was published when she was about 9 years old. A long poem about Jesus feeding the 5,000, it appeared in the office paper where her father worked.

Nina loves to write and has had 40 books and almost 300 stories published. She has eight children and five grandchildren and says that God has been very good to her, giving her lots of stories to write and people to love.

Colleen L. Reece lived in the woods of Washington State when she was a child. Her home was so far out of town that the family had no electricity, so Colleen learned to read under the warm yellow glow of a kerosene lamp.

Colleen always wanted to write books, and she accepted the Lord Jesus into her heart when she was just a little girl.

Many years later God answered Colleen's prayers. She has had nearly 60 books published, including *JumpStart*; *Sandwich Island Summer*; *The Mysterious Treadle Machine*; *Plain, Plain Melissa Jane*; and *PK the Great*. She has had articles published in many magazines, including *Vibrant Life*, *Signs of the Times*, and *Our Little Friend*.

After a career as a pastor's wife and an O.B. nurse, **Lynn Ripley** went back to school, graduating from Southwestern Adventist College with a B.A. in theology. She is principal of Mountain State Academy in Pennsboro, West Virginia. Her stories are drawn from experiences with her three children: Jimi, Heather, and David II.

Marjorie Kidder Snyder graduated from Indiana Academy and Emmanuel Missionary College. In addition to being a pastor's wife for 35 years, she has also been involved in giving camp meeting workshops. In 1983 she was elected to serve as the children's ministries director and in 1989 communications director of the Michigan Conference of Seventh-day Adventists. Marjorie has been published in 16 denominational publications.

Carol Barron Thomas was editorial secretary for *Message* magazine when she wrote these stories. She cherishes memories of growing up in New Jersey with her four brothers and three sisters. "My parents, Edward and Cora Barron, played with us," Carol says. "Daddy taught me how to skate and play baseball."

Carol, whose husband, Clarence L. Thomas III, is an ordained minister, is the mother of three grown children, Clarence IV, Donna-Maria, and Torrence. The Thomases were missionaries for 12 years in Brazil and the Caribbean, and Carol writes about some of their experiences.

Beverly Hill-Velting makes her living as a "creative entrepreneur," taking assignments for varied art projects, commercial and freelance writing, word processing, and desktop publishing. Since she was 12 years old she has worked with children in various Sabbath school departments. She created the "Winner Kids" picture story series, which ran monthly in *The Winner* for nine years. Beverly has two daughters and had a son, Gayland, who was killed in an auto accident when he was only 15. Her love for Gayland, who had a remarkable talent for writing, has been her inspiration to hone her own writing ability and to reach out to young people of all ages.

VeraLee Wiggins lives in College Place, Washington, with her husband and granddaughter, Julie. She has four grown children and seven grandchildren.

VeraLee loves animals almost more than anything else, especially the family Pomeranian, Little Lady Nika Fantasia, also known as Bunky. VeraLee takes lots of pictures, mostly of Julie and Bunky. She also enjoys music. She and her husband have music in their office all the time as they work. In the spring the family eagerly waits for good weather so that they can pile into their pickup and fifth-wheel camper for weekends of fun and relaxation.

Family Worship

activities for preschoolers

Beautiful Feet

NEEDED: two sheets of construction paper—one black, one blue; a sheet of poster board; scissors; glue; pen.

Help your child trace his or her feet on the colored construction paper. Attach the black paper and cut out two sets of footprints at the same time. Mount the footprints on the poster board, placing one set of footprints beneath and a little to one side of the other set, making a shadow effect.

Let's all look at our feet. Everybody, take off your socks and shoes.

Our feet are very important. It would be hard to walk and run without them. Our leg bone ends at our ankles. Can you wiggle your ankle up and down and sideways? Where's your heel? Arch? Instep? Ball? How do your toes help you? Can you pick up something with them? Everyone's feet are different, but they help us in many of the same ways.

The Bible says that some feet are beautiful. Do you know what makes them that way? "How lovely on the mountains are the feet of the herald who comes to . . . bring good news, . . . calling to Zion, 'Your God is king!' " (Isa. 52:7, NEB).

Everyone is excited to see someone bringing good things. When someone brings you a package, or when you've been waiting extra long for Mom or Dad, isn't it exciting to see them come up the walk? You may not have looked particularly at their feet, but your parents probably looked wonderful all over, even their feet.

Isaiah says that when we tell other people the good news about God, our feet are beautiful. Let's write this verse from Isaiah on the picture of your footprints, to help

us remember how good it is to be God's messenger. —
C.W.H.

Lost!

NEEDED: stuffed animal for a younger child; quarter for an older one.
Before it's time for your devotional period with your family, hide a toy or a quarter for each child.

Sometimes we lose things that are very important to us. Have you ever lost a shoe or boot, and everybody in the family had to help you find it before you could go out? I have. I feel awful when I really need something and I can't find it, don't you?

I've hidden something for each one of you to find. (*Tell your children what you've hidden for them so that they know what they are looking for, and let them find it.*)

Jesus knows how happy we are when we find something we've lost. He told two stories about people who had lost something they wanted very much. One story was about a man who had lost a lamb. The other story was about a woman who had lost a silver coin. The man and woman were so happy when they found their lost things that they called their friends and neighbors to come and be happy with them.

Jesus said, "In the same way, I tell you, there is joy among the angels of God over one sinner who repents" (Luke 15:10, NEB). You see, God and His angels love you very much. When you say that you are sorry for the wrong things you have done and you want to be God's friend again, they are *so* glad. They feel like they have found someone very precious who was lost and found again — you! — C.W.H.

When God Dresses the Flowers

NEEDED: real flowers, colored tissue paper or crepe paper, toothpicks, glue, pipe cleaners (optional: picture of King Solomon).

Show your child how to cut the paper into 2″ x 10″ strips. Spread glue along one long edge of a strip. Gather the glued edge of the strip around and around one end of the pipe cleaner, to form the shape of a flower—each strip will make one flower. If you have green paper, cut out leaves and glue them to the pipe cleaner stem.

You may want to make enough flowers for a bouquet. Compare your paper flowers to real flowers.

The flowers we make are pretty, but God's flowers are even prettier! Jesus said, "Think about how the lilies grow in the fields. They don't work; they don't make clothes. But I tell you, even Solomon with all his beautiful kingly robes, was not as nicely dressed as one of these lilies" (Matt. 6:28, 29, paraphrased).

Jesus says that if God can take such good care of flowers, which don't last very long, don't you think He'll take care of you? God must love flowers, because He made so many beautiful ones. But God loves you even more! When you get dressed, you can remember how God is taking care of you and thank Him!—C.W.H.

Shining Like the Sun

NEEDED: a sunny, pleasantly warm day if you will have your devotions outside, or a bright window.

11

Everyone, close your eyes and feel the sun shining on you. Remember not to look at the sun because it will burn your eyes. How does the sun make your skin feel? How does it make you feel inside? What do you think the sun is like?

Now, while you are feeling the sun, listen to something Jesus said. He had been telling His friends a story about when He was going to send His angels to gather everyone and everything that has made our world bad and burn them.

Then Jesus said that something very beautiful would happen. "The righteous will shine like the sun in the kingdom of their Father" (Matt. 13:43, RSV).

Why do you think Jesus said we would be like the sun? The sun is so bright, it makes our world full of light, even though it is very far away. It makes us feel good and warm, and it helps the plants grow.

God's people will be like the sun because they will help everyone around them feel warm and good too! God will fill them so full of happiness and goodness that they will shine!

It will be wonderful to shine like the sun, won't it? When you feel the warm sun, you can always remember that Jesus will make you shine as warm and bright, when He comes again. —C.W.H.

Simon Says

We're going to play a game called "Simon Says." Everybody stand up!

(Proceed to give instructions such as "Simon says grab your ankles," "Simon says wave your hands over your head," etc. If you have older preschoolers, omit "Simon says" every once in a while and give only the directions—

they must sit down if they do something without "Simon" telling them to. This is a good time to review names of parts of the body, such as elbows, knees, wrists, and hips. After everyone has had a good time but interest is still high, calm the children with commands such as "Simon says to run your thumb softly from your head to your toes" and "Simon says to sink into a quiet heap on the floor." Then say, "Simon says to put on your listening caps as I read something from the Bible about our game.")

"Lord, You have searched me and You know me. You know when I sit down and when I stand up. You know when I go out and when I lie down. You know every word I'm going to say before I say it" (Ps. 139:1-4, paraphrased).

We did lots of things in our game. Do you think God knows what we did? Of course He does! *(Whisper "I love you!" in your child's ear.)* Do you think God knows what I said to you? Yes, of course! Wherever we go today, and whatever we do, let's remember that God is watching us and helping us and loving us. —C.W.H.

Writing a Family Psalm

NEEDED: pencil and paper

Psalm 136 has a nice pattern that we can use to write a family history psalm. This psalm tells a story about how God helped His people. I'll read the first part of the story, and then you all say, "His love goes on forever." After we read the psalm the way it is written in the Bible, we'll make up our own verses.

"It is good to give thanks to the Lord,
His love goes on forever.

Give thanks to Him."
"He struck down the firstborn of the Egyptians,
His love goes on forever.
And brought Israel out from among them;
His love goes on forever.
With strong hand and outstretched arm —
His love goes on forever —
He divided the Red Sea in two —
His love goes on forever —
and made Israel pass through it;
His love goes on forever.
But Pharaoh and his host He swept into the Red Sea;
His love goes on forever.''
—Psalm 136:1, 2, 10-15 (paraphrased)

Each of us can think of something that God has done for us. We'll go around the circle. One of us will say a sentence about how God has helped us, and then we'll all say "His love goes on forever."

[You may want to close your family psalm with the last verse of Psalm 136: "Give thanks to the God of heaven, for his love goes on forever."]—C.W.H.

Sleeping in Peace

Let's pretend that this finger [your child's pointer finger] is you, and your other hand is your bed. Now watch me, and do what I do!
This little boy [girl] is going to bed.
Down on the pillow he [she] lays his [her] head
(*lay thumb down for pillow, and rest the pointer finger on it*).
Wraps himself [herself] in the covers so tight

14

(cover pointer finger with four fingers),
And this is the way he [she] sleeps all night.
Morning comes. He [she] opens his [her] eyes
(close and open your eyes).
Back with a toss the covers fly
(open the four fingers).
Up he [she] jumps, is dressed and away
(stand pointer finger up and make it hop up and down),
Ready for fun and frolic all day!

You are very special to God, and He loves to take care of you! The Bible says, "I go to bed and sleep in peace. Lord, only you keep me safe" (Ps. 4:8, ICB).

Sometimes we are afraid when the wind shakes our house and it's stormy outside. Sometimes we hear scary noises, or see scary shadows. When you are scared, say this verse over and over. It will help you feel that God is close by, keeping you safe. —C.W.H.

Rainbows

NEEDED: clear glass of water, large white paper, sunshine coming through a window.

Rainbows make us feel good when we see them! You can make a rainbow by filling a glass with water and placing it in a sunny window. Let the edge of the glass extend over the edge of the sill, but be careful not to let the glass fall! Put the white piece of paper on the floor under the sill. When the light shines through the water, you should see a rainbow on the paper.

God must love rainbows, because He uses them in some very important places. The Bible says that God's throne in heaven has a rainbow around it "bright as an emerald" (Rev. 4:3, NEB).

15

In another place the Bible describes a mighty angel coming down from heaven. "He was wrapped in cloud, with the rainbow round his head; his face shone like the sun and his legs were like pillars of fire" (Rev. 10:1, NEB).

Where have you last seen a rainbow? Do you remember when God put the first rainbow in the sky? God put it there after the Flood. It was a promise to Noah and his family that God was watching over the world and that it would never again be covered with a flood.

When we see a rainbow, it can remind us of the rainbow around God's throne, the rainbow over the angel's head, and God's promise to take care of us. It can help us think about how wonderful God is to share with us such a beautiful part of heaven. —C.W.H.

Building on Rock

NEEDED: a pillow; a smooth, solid surface, such as a floor or table; wooden building blocks.

Do you remember the story that Jesus told about the two men who built houses—one on the sand and one on the rock? (If you know the song "The Wise Man Built His House on the Rock," sing it with your child.)

We're going to do an experiment to show why foundations are so important. First, we need to build a house on the floor [or table]. Do you remember how you built it from these blocks? Next, let's build the same kind of house on this pillow. Is the house on the pillow staying up very well? What if we push down on the pillow a little? What do you think is the trouble?

Jesus says that we need to build on a solid, firm foundation so that our building will stay up. "Surely you know that you are God's temple, where the Spirit of God dwells" (1 Cor. 3:16, NEB). You see, we are the building. And do you know what we need to build on for a strong foundation? Jesus is our foundation! He's our rock!

That's why we need to listen carefully to everything that He says, and obey Him. That way we won't crash like the house on the pillow! —C.W.H.

Windows of Heaven

Needed: large cardboard box (large enough for your child to sit inside), knife.

Help your child into the box and ask, "What can you see when you are hiding inside that box? It feels pretty dark and lonely in there, doesn't it?"

Get out for a moment, and I'll cut a window in the top of the box. (*Cut three sides of a square so that the window can close again.*) Now you can get back in the box. It's dark with the window closed, but when we open it, all of a sudden there is light! It doesn't seem so lonely anymore, does it! You can see me, and I can see you.

God said that He would open the windows in the sky for us. "Bring the tithes into the treasury . . . ; let there be food in my house. Put me to the proof, says the Lord of Hosts, and see if I do not open windows in the sky and pour a blessing on you as long as there is a need" (Mal. 3:10, NEB).

God doesn't want us to forget to return to Him the tithes that belong to Him. When we return them, He will open the windows in the sky, and we will feel just like you did in the box, when you could see out the window. We will be happier and feel closer to God, and He will bless what we have. —C.W.H.

Apples of Gold

NEEDED: silver tinsel or aluminum foil cut in narrow strips; gold foil or paper (from Christmas cards or wrapping paper), or a gold crayon and paper; spray adhesive; tacky glue; clear or white glitter; piece of poster board.

Once God asked young King Solomon what he would like best in the world. Solomon could have asked for anything—ships, beautiful horses, or big houses full of wonderful things. But do you know what he asked for? He asked God to make him wise. He wanted to know the right things to do and say. God was so pleased with Solomon that He made him rich, too!

Solomon knew that saying the right thing at the right time is very important. One of the wise things he said was that good words are as valuable as "apples of gold in a setting of silver" (Prov. 25:11, RSV).

God can help you choose good words to say, just like He helped King Solomon. He loves to do things like that for you! Saying "Please" and "Thank you" and things that help people feel good about themselves and God are wise words.

We can make a picture of gold apples on a silver background that will help us remember how important wise words are.

(Spray the poster board with adhesive. Lay the tinsel in stripes diagonally across the paper—tinsel, space, tinsel, etc. Lay more stripes in the opposite diagonal direction, to make a checkerboard pattern. Sprinkle glitter on the picture, and shake off the excess glitter.

(Cut out three gold apples. Cut out gold leaves and stems, and glue the apples and leaves and stems on the

18

silver checkerboard. Write the verse below the apples if you like.) —C.W.H.

Listening With Our Heart

NEEDED: cans or plastic containers with lids (such as ready-made icing comes in); noise-making materials such as rice, nuts and bolts, gravel, sand, etc.

Make listening cans by filling one pair with rice, another pair with nuts and bolts, etc. Try to make at least three pairs of cans. Mix the cans, and see if your child can match the pairs of cans that sound the same.

Learning to listen is one of the most important things we can do. Do you remember the story of King Solomon? He asked God to help him be wise. But he didn't say "Please help me be wise." He said "Give [your] servant . . . a heart with skill to listen" (1 Kings 3:9, NEB). Solomon wanted a heart that knew how to listen.

You were listening very carefully to the different sounds in the cans in order to match them. We need to listen to people, too. Mom and Dad have important things to tell you, and you need to be able not only to *hear* us with your ears, but to *understand* us with your heart. But of course, even more than listening to Mom and Dad, you need to know how to listen to God.

When Samuel was a little boy and God wanted to talk to him, God called and called. At first Samuel didn't know who was calling to him! But when he found out it was God, he said, "Speak, Lord, for your servant is listening" (1 Sam. 3:9, NIV).

Perhaps you can tell God that you are listening too—listening with your heart—to hear what He has to say.—C.W.H.

Invisible Salt

NEEDED: two clear glasses, salt, warm water, saucer. Fill both glasses one fourth full of warm water. Let your child pour in several teaspoons of salt and stir until the salt is dissolved.

Can you see any salt in the water? (*If all the salt won't dissolve, pour in a little more warm water and stir until it does.*) Do you think the salt is still in the water, or do you think it is gone? Taste the water in both glasses. Is the salt still in the glass we poured it into? We can't see the salt, but we can taste it.

Let's pour the salt solution out into this saucer. The water will evaporate into the air, and we'll see what happens to the salt. What do you think will happen?

When Jesus is in our heart, other people can't see Him there. But they know He is there because of the loving things we do! The Bible says, "If there is this love among you, then all will know that you are my disciples" (John 13:35, NEB).

The Jesus love in our heart shows when we say kind, helpful things. It shows when we do things for others without them even asking us. When people see us smiling, and they see the kind and loving things we do, they know Jesus is our friend, even though they can't see Him.—C.W.H.

Wheel of Love

NEEDED: a wheel with centered spokes, such as a wagon or tricycle.

Just about everything we see in this world can help us understand more about God. Even this wheel can help us!

The outside of the wheel is called the rim. Spokes go from the rim to the center hub of the wheel. Have you noticed what happens to the spokes as they come toward the center of the wheel? They get closer to each other!

Now, let's imagine that God is here, at the center of the wheel. This spoke is Daddy, getting closer to God. This spoke is you, getting closer to God. We may be far apart out here, away from God, but the closer we come to God, the closer we come to each other!

The Bible says, "When we love God and obey his commands we love his children too" (1 John 5:2, NEB). This is God's way of bringing peace and love to our world. The more we love God, the more He can fill our hearts with love for each other.

People who love each other won't want to hurt each other or make each other angry. They want to make each other happy, instead! What a wonderful world we would have if we all tried to make each other happy. Can you think of some things you want to do today?—C.W.H.

Talking Without Words

We are going to play a game. I'm going to try to tell you something without using any words. See if you can tell what I'm saying!

(Make motions that communicate ideas such as Come here, I'm cold, I'm hot, I've lost something, Look over there, I'm proud of you, I don't know, I like this, I'm excited, I'm sad, I'm tired. When you've played the game several times, give everyone a chance to communicate nonverbally.)

What parts of your body did you use to let us know what you were thinking? You probably used all of your body at one time or another! What parts of your body did you use most?

We have many ways of telling people things without using words. We put lights in our windows and wreaths on our front door to wish people Merry Christmas. We wear our best clean clothes when we go to church, to let God know we think He is very special and important.

God tells us things without using words, too. He made the birds, and when they sing we can feel the joyful feelings God put into their hearts. When we see the beautiful trees, butterflies, flowers, mountains, and snow, we feel God's power. We know He loves beautiful things. And we can tell that He loves us, even though He doesn't say it out loud, because He made so many good things for us.

"The pastures are filled with flocks of sheep, and the valleys are carpeted with grain. All the world shouts with joy, and sings" (Ps. 65:13, TLB). —C.W.H.

Shining in the Dark

NEEDED: aluminum foil, dark-colored construction paper, tape or glue.

Did you know that the Bible says we shouldn't grumble and argue? That sounds just like what Mom and Dad say! This is what the Bible says to do instead—"Shine like stars in a dark world" (Phil. 2:15, NEB).

Grumbling and arguing make our dark world darker and darker. But when Mom or Dad asks you to do something and you smile and say "OK! I'll do that!" you make a bright happy spot in our world, just like a star!

Let's make a picture of stars shining in the dark to remind us to be cheerful and happy.

(Fold the construction paper in several places and help your child cut out a variety of starlike shapes. Attach a sheet of aluminum foil to the back of the construction paper and let the stars shine through. You might want to write the verse somewhere on the picture as well.) —C.W.H.

A Sweet-smelling Parade

NEEDED: perfume.

We are going to have a parade! It will be Jesus' victory parade because all of us who are marching in it belong to Him. The Bible talks about what our parade is for: "Thanks be to God, who always leads us in victory through Christ. God uses us to spread his knowledge everywhere like a sweet-smelling perfume" (2 Cor. 2:14, ICB).

God wants us to spread around the fragrance of God's goodness. Do you know what fragrance is? It is perfume. When someone has perfume or aftershave cologne on, she or he often leaves a little bit of the odor in the air around her or him. We know that person has been around because the air smells so good.

That's how God wants us to be. He wants us to spread around good things about Him. When we tell people about the things God has done that make us happy, it's like spreading perfume about God!

First, let's each say something about what God has done to make us happy today. Then we'll put on some of this perfume and have a parade around the living room. We can sing a happy song about God while we march! — C.W.H.

Jesus' Lamb

NEEDED: snipped pieces of mop strands or pieces of toilet tissue, poster board, tacky glue, black craft acrylic paint [optional: red ribbon and small bell].

Jesus liked to tell stories about sheep because there were so many on the hills where the people came to listen to Him. Jesus told stories about lambs getting lost and about wolves and robbers trying to get them.

Jesus knew how much sheep need someone to watch over them. And to Him, the people listening to His stories were like sheep because they needed a shepherd to care for them, too.

"I am your shepherd," He told them. "I am the good shepherd; I know my own sheep and my sheep know me . . . and I lay down my life for the sheep" (John 10:14, NEB).

Do you remember that song that tells us that Jesus is the shepherd? Do you remember who you are in the song? Yes, you are Jesus' little lamb. Let's sing that song.

Jesus loves to take care of you, for you belong to Him! Let's make a lamb to help us remember that Jesus is our shepherd.

(Cut a lamb shape from a piece of poster board. Paint the muzzle and legs black, and glue on snips of mop or crumpled

24

pieces of tissue for wool. Tie a red ribbon and a bell around the sheep's neck, if you like.) —C.W.H.

Jesus and the Cross

[The next three devotionals are designed to be done together, over a weekend.]
NEEDED: a shoe box, sand or dirt, twigs or Popsicle sticks, thread or twine, paper, pencil, 1″ x 12″ strip of tissue paper, small block of wood, stone, red tape to seal "tomb."

When Jesus the Good Shepherd said He would lay down His life for His sheep, He meant that He would die. An enemy, Satan, was trying to kill us. Satan said that since we were so bad, we belonged to him, and he could kill us. But Jesus said that He would take our place. He would die instead of us.

That's why Jesus let the soldiers put Him on the cross. He could have stopped them from hurting Him, but He didn't. He died for us, His precious sheep, because He didn't want us to belong to the enemy.

Let's make a cross like the one Jesus died on. *(Tie the twigs or Popsicle sticks together in the shape of a cross.)* Now you can draw a picture of Jesus to put on the cross.

The Bible says "The soldiers took charge of Jesus. Carrying his own cross, Jesus went out to a place called The Place of the Skull. . . . There they nailed Jesus to the cross" (John 19:16-18, ICB). *(Help your child act this out, as Jesus drags the cross to the shoe box of dirt. Lay Jesus on the cross and attach Him with a little glue or sticky tack.)*

Pilate had a paper fastened to the cross. It read "Jesus of Nazareth, King of the Jews." *(Attach a similar paper to your cross.)* Then Jesus died. Two of Jesus' friends took His body down from the cross. They wrapped it and put it in the tomb. *(Wrap Jesus in the strip of tissue paper. Place Him on a block. Cut a door in a shoe box and turn the box upside down over Jesus. Place a stone and the red tape at the entrance to the tomb.)*

Jesus' friends went sadly home. The sun went down, and it was Sabbath. We are going to let Jesus rest in His tomb over Sabbath, just like the real Jesus did when He died for us long ago. —C.W.H.

When Jesus Rested on the Sabbath

NEEDED: paper and crayons, or clay.
Let your child make something out of the paper or clay.

What you made is very nice. When our world was new, just finished, Jesus looked at everything He had made. He thought it was very good, too! The Bible says, "By the seventh day God finished the work he had been doing. So on the seventh day he rested from all his work. God blessed the seventh day and made it a holy day. He made it holy because on that day he rested. He rested from all the work he had done in creating the world" (Gen. 2:2, 3, ICB).

Adam and Eve kept the Sabbath, and people who love God have kept the Sabbath day every week since then. But Jesus had more work to do. The enemy, Satan, made the beautiful, good world into a big, bad mess, and we are part of the mess. Jesus was the only one who could fix it, because He made us.

In order to fix the mess, Jesus came down to this world and died. Just before He died on the cross, He cried, "It is finished." Then He rested again, just like He rested after He had made the world. He rested all Sabbath long.

When we keep the Sabbath like Jesus did, it helps us remember two things. We remember when Jesus made the world and us. And we remember that Jesus died for us, so that we could belong to Him instead of the enemy, Satan.

It's like this picture you made. It's yours, isn't it? But what if someone bad took it away? "You have to pay me to get it back," that person said. So you gave him all your money, and bought your picture back. It would be yours twice. It would be yours because you made it, and it would be yours because you bought it.

That's how it is with Jesus. We belong to Him because He made us *and* because He bought us back from the wicked enemy, Satan, by dying for us on the cross. — C.W.H.

When Jesus Rose From the Grave

NEEDED: heavy paper, pencil, sealed tomb with Jesus inside [soldiers outside of the tomb are optional].
Help your child make several angels, three women, and Peter and John, who will visit the tomb.

The Bible says, "It's very important that I tell you this story, how Jesus died for our sins, like the Bible said He would; how Jesus was buried; and how He was raised to life on the third day, just like the Bible said would happen" (1 Cor. 15:3, 4, paraphrased).

Remember how Jesus rested in the tomb all Sabbath? The next day was Sunday. Early in the morning there was a big earthquake. An angel came down from heaven. He broke the seal on the tomb and rolled the stone away from the doorway to the tomb. The soldiers guarding the tomb fell down like they were dead. Maybe the angel unwrapped Jesus and helped Him fold up the grave clothes. We don't know, because the soldiers were too afraid to look and see. (*Unwrap Jesus, fold up the tissues, lay them neatly inside the tomb, and seat the angel on the stone.*)

But we do know that Jesus walked out of that tomb alive! When the women came to take care of Jesus' body, an angel was sitting on the stone. "Don't be afraid," he told the women. "I know you are looking for Jesus, but He isn't here. Come see where He was laid in the tomb, and then go tell His friends that He has been raised from the dead!"

Mary Magdalene, Joanna, and Mary, mother of James, ran to tell Peter and John. Peter and John ran to the tomb as fast as they could go, and they saw that Jesus was gone. (*Help your child use the paper figures to act these scenes out.*) They went home again, but Mary Magdalene stayed by the tomb. She was crying.

Mary looked into the tomb again, and she saw two angels, one sitting where Jesus' head had been and one sitting where His feet had been. How the angels must have loved Jesus, and how glad they must have been to see Him alive again! They must have felt very sorry for Mary, because they asked her why she was crying.

She said, "They have taken my Lord away, and I don't know where they have laid Him." Then she turned around and saw Jesus, but she was crying so hard she didn't even know it was He!

Jesus asked her why she was crying. Mary thought Jesus was the gardener, and she asked Him if He had taken Jesus away. Then Jesus said, "Mary!" and Mary knew it was really Jesus standing there, her very best friend.

"Teacher!" she cried. What a happy time that was! Jesus told Mary to tell all His friends that He was going back to His Father. "I have seen the Lord!" Mary said over and over as she gave each of His friends His message.

Jesus did go back to heaven to His Father, and He's getting ready for us to live there with Him! But right now, He wants us to tell this story to our friends like Mary did. He wants us to tell them that He is alive and that He loves them!—C.W.H.

Fastened Like a Peg

NEEDED: nail or peg; board into which the nail can be driven to support weight; hammer; nonbreakable items to hang from the nail, such as pans, aprons, cups.

Help your child drive the nail or peg into the board, and hang a number of things on the nail.

We use hooks and nails and pegs to help us keep our house organized. What things do we have hanging up in our kitchen? Our bathroom? The garage? Our closets?

The Bible talks about a very important peg being fastened up on a wall. All kinds of beautiful pots and pans and bowls were hanging from this peg. But then the peg that was holding up all those dishes fell. And what do you think happened to the pots and pans and bowls? (*Loosen the peg or nail, or tilt the board, letting everything hanging on it fall.*) It made a terrible crash. All the beautiful pots and pans broke into pieces. They were totally ruined.

We are like that peg. Did you know that people need you? Your friends and your brothers and sisters depend on you, like those pans depended on the nail to hold them up. If you do something that you know isn't right, your friends may copy you. Then all of you may go crashing down.

Listen to what God says. "I shall fasten him firmly in place like a peg. On him will hang the whole glory of the family" (Isa. 22:23, 24, REB)—even the smallest pots and pans. I hope He's talking about you! If you let Him, God will help you be careful to do what is right. You will be stuck firmly in the wall, and everyone who knows you can depend on you.—C.W.H.

Which Pot Are You?

NEEDED: a variety of household containers— beautiful gold, silver, pewter, brass, copper or porcelain pots or vases, cooking pots, clay pots, paper and plastic throwaways, tin cans.

We have lots of different kinds of containers in our house. Some of them are very cheap, and we usually don't keep them long. When we empty the food from the tin cans, we usually throw them away. If Dad is going to change the oil in the car, he usually finds some cheap container he can leave at the recycling center to put the oil in. Or if Mom needs something to hold paint or glue, she looks for something she doesn't mind getting messed up.

But what happens when it is Sabbath, and we want a pretty vase and flowers on the table? Maybe company is coming, and we want to have a nice dinner. We get out our best vase for the flowers, and we choose our nicest dishes to put the olives and salad and dessert in!

In the Bible, Paul writes about all the kinds of containers in homes. "In a wealthy home there are dishes made of gold and silver as well as some made from wood and clay.

The expensive dishes are used for guests, and the cheap ones are used in the kitchen or to put garbage in. If you stay away from sin you will be like one of these dishes made of purest gold—the very best in the house—so that Christ himself can use you for his highest purposes" (2 Tim. 2:20, 21, TLB).

I want to be a special container that Jesus can use for His most important jobs, don't you? We can ask Him to clean us all up and make us into a wonderful dish of gold that He can use. —C.W.H.

Poured Out

NEEDED: a pitcher that your child can handle, your child's favorite juice, cups, paper with child's name, tape.

Something yummy is in this pitcher. What do you think it is? Why do you think it's in here? The juice is in here to share! We are going to pretend that this pitcher is you. Write your name on this paper, and we'll stick it on the pitcher. But before we pour anything out of you, let's read what the Bible says about what is inside you.

"This precious treasure—this light and power that now shine within us—is held in a perishable container, that is, in our weak bodies. Everyone can see that the glorious power within [us] must be from God and is not our own" (2 Cor. 4:7, TLB).

The Bible says that all the good things inside you that you can share with others are precious treasures! We know that this pitcher didn't make this juice. You didn't make all the good things in you, either. Who did? God did, of course! All your happy smiles, all the good things you say and do for other people, come from God! He gives these things to you to share with other people!

Now you can share the juice in your pitcher. And then we'll all thank God for the wonderful things He's given to you so that you can share them with us! —C.W.H.

Salt and Pepper

NEEDED: saucer, salt, finely ground pepper, plastic pen or comb, wool felt or material.

Mix a little salt and pepper on the saucer. Show your child how to rub the pen or comb very hard with the wool material. Hold the pen or comb close to the plate and pass it slowly over the salt and pepper. The pepper should jump up to the pen and leave the salt behind. If you hold the pen too close, the salt also will be attracted by the static electricity in the pen or comb.

This experiment reminds me of a story in the Bible that Jesus told. He said that the kingdom of heaven is like a field that a farmer sowed with good wheat seed. While the farmer was sleeping, an enemy came and sowed weed seeds in with the wheat. When the wheat came up, the weeds came up too.

The farmer's helpers went to their boss and said, "Sir, didn't you plant wheat? Where did the weeds come from?"

The farmer said, "An enemy did this."

"Do you want us to pull out all the weeds now?" his men asked.

The farmer shook his head. "No, because when you pull up the weeds, you might also pull up the wheat. Let the weeds and the wheat grow together until the harvest time. At harvest time I will tell the workers this: First gather the weeds and tie them together to be burned. Then gather the wheat and bring it to my barn" (Matt. 13:29, 30, ICB).

Jesus explained that our world is the field and that we are the wheat He has planted. There are also weeds in the world—people who do what's wrong and don't want to love Jesus. Sometimes we wonder why Jesus lets these bad people be here where they can make so many problems for us.

We know that someday Jesus will separate the good people from the bad people, just like we separated the pepper from the salt. But it isn't time to do that yet. He wants to make sure He doesn't lose any wheat! He wants to make sure that all the people who want to come to heaven get a chance to find out about Him. —C.W.H.

Before We Were Born

NEEDED: pictures of prenatal development, sono-gram of your child, or record of a heartbeat.

These are some pictures of how you looked when you were a teeny, tiny little something inside of Mommy. You were even too tiny to be called a baby! You started off as a little speck so small that no one could see you. You grew and grew. You slept and played and grew some more, until you were ready to be born.

Do you know who made you? The Bible says it was God. "You made my whole being. You formed me in my mother's body. I praise you because you made me in an amazing and wonderful way. What you have done is wonderful. I know this very well. You saw my bones being formed as I took shape in my mother's body. When I was put together there, you saw my body as it was formed" (Ps. 139:13-15, ICB).

Even Mom didn't know what you were going to be like! But you weren't a secret to God. God knew just how you would look, and what you were going to be like, and He loved you.

Let's praise God for making you, shall we? Do you want to draw a picture or sing a song to tell God how glad you are that He is so wonderful? He loves to hear us thank Him! — C.W.H.

Stories for Growing

More Than You Ask

Now to Him who is able to do exceedingly abundantly above all that we ask or think. Eph. 3:20, NKJV.

Putt, putt, putt went the old car down the snow-covered roads to church every Wednesday night to prayer meeting and every Sabbath to Sabbath school and church.

The heater in the car didn't work anymore.

Nicole, Lakisha, Bill, Mom, and Dad all snuggled together, with their legs wrapped in blankets to keep warm.

Dad prayed to God that he could get enough money and enough time to fix up that old car.

Well, time passed, and Dad never had the time or money to fix up the car. But about a year later a woman called on the telephone. Dad had met her earlier. This woman wanted to meet the entire family and help them. She invited the family to go for a ride. This ride was to a company that sold cars.

At the car dealer's the woman said, "Do you see that car over there?" She pointed to a brand-new light-tan Buick LeSabre. "The dealer left the car unlocked for us, so let's get out and look at it."

Nicole, Lakisha, Bill, Mom, and Dad all jumped out of the woman's car. They went to the new car and sat on the plush cloth seats. Their eyes bulged with excitement.

The woman looked at Dad and said, "I don't like the color of this car, but if you like it, it's yours. I will buy it and give it to you."

At first Dad was speechless. Then he blurted out, "I like it; the color's fine!" And so they got a new car.

Sometimes God gives us more than we ask or think. Our God is a "BIG GOD!" He wants to do something "BIG" for you. —E.G.N.

Cut It Out

He who overcomes shall inherit all things. Rev. 21:7, NKJV.

Dorothy sat watching a group of pigeons fly by her window and land on the ground. They were looking for little bits of food to eat. She discovered that one poor pigeon's feet were so tangled that it could hardly walk. But whenever Dorothy tried to catch the pigeon, it would fly away. Maybe the pigeon didn't know that Dorothy really wanted to help it.

I've got a plan! she thought. So she took a cardboard box, made a flap for an entrance, and placed burlap on top with a long string attached. On the floor of the box she placed a few pieces of corn. Then she sat back and held the string.

Slowly the pigeon made its way into the box. Dorothy gave a quick pull on the string. The burlap went down and caught the bird. Dorothy and her friend carefully cut away the string and wire that had gotten tangled around the pigeon's feet, making its life so hard and painful. Dorothy watched happily as the bird flew away to freedom.

But after that, whenever all the birds flew down to the ground by the window to eat, the rescued pigeon would fly very close to Dorothy. The bird seemed to understand why Dorothy had wanted to catch it.

When I think about that bird whose feet were so tangled, it reminds me of people who get tangled in sin. Just as Dorothy had a plan to help the bird, so Jesus has a plan to help us. Sometimes He needs to catch us and cut away things in our lives that would keep us from going to heaven! —P.H.

A Special Gift to Jesus

Jesus was born in Bethlehem in Judea. Matt. 2:1, NIV.

Have you ever thought about giving a special gift to Jesus?

It was Christmastime, and Yolanda wanted to give Jesus a gift. "Mommy, what gift can I give to Jesus? My doll, or my *Baby Moses* book? Would Jesus come for it?"

Mother said, "I love you, Yolanda, and I'm happy that you love Jesus."

"How do you know I love Jesus?" Yolanda asked.

"Well, you want to give Him a gift, and you talk about Him often."

"But maybe I shouldn't give Him my doll. He probably doesn't want a doll or a book. I don't know what to give Him."

Hugging her daughter, Mother said, "Yolanda, the best gift you can give to Jesus is your heart!"

"How can I give Jesus my heart? It's inside my chest."

Mother smiled. "Yolanda, I mean that you can let Jesus know you want to be like Him and do the things He wants you to do."

"How can I be like Jesus, Mommy?"

"By being a good girl in Sabbath school, by picking up your toys, by helping with your baby sister, and by telling your friends about Jesus."

"Jesus will know that I love Him, 'cause I want to be just like Him. I'm going to give Him my heart right now!"—A.C.B.

I Still Remember It!

To obey is better than sacrifice. 1 Sam. 15:22.

When I was little we lived in the big city of New Orleans. Every day a man came around with ice for sale. We didn't have a refrigerator, so we would buy a big block of ice and put it in our icebox to keep our food cold.

Kids would race to the truck to see who could hop onto it first to get the little pieces of ice on the floor of the truck. My grandmother told me not to get up there because I was too little and might get hurt.

Well, it was hot, and I wanted a piece of ice to suck on, so I got my little feet in the right places and climbed onto the truck. I found a big piece of ice and was ready to get down when I slipped on a small piece of ice and fell on my face. I bumped my forehead, nose, and chin. The driver carried me to my grandmother. She took care of my cuts and bruises but didn't say anything. She knew I had disobeyed. She just looked hurt.

That was a long time ago. But I still remember it! Now I am an adult, and I try to remember what Jesus wants me to do. I don't want to get hurt to remind me to obey. —A.C.B.

The Birdnapper

Be careful—watch out for attacks from Satan, your great enemy. 1 Peter 5:8, TLB.

One day Billy found four eggs in the birdhouse that he and Daddy had built.

"Do you think you can wait two weeks before you bother the mother bird again?" Daddy asked Billy. Billy waited, but it was very hard.

Finally, Daddy helped Billy check the nest again. "Sh-h-h," Billy whispered. "We don't want to scare the babies."

They quietly opened the top of the birdhouse and found four tiny almost-hairless birds. When the babies heard Billy, they all opened their mouths. "They want you to give them a bug," Daddy whispered.

Two days later, Billy discovered there were only three baby birds!

The next day only two baby birds huddled in the nest. In tears, Billy ran into the house.

"Why don't you watch and see what's getting your little birds?" Daddy asked.

Later Billy saw their old Siamese cat, Thor, climb the post to the birdhouse. Billy snatched the big cat down from the post. He carried him to the house.

Daddy cut open a piece of stove pipe. Then he and Billy nailed it around the post. "You see," Daddy said, "Thor won't be able to get a grip on this metal. If he tries to climb up to the birds, he'll just slide back down." He looked at Billy. "Thor is sort of like the old devil, Satan, isn't he? Satan goes around trying to hurt things. It was easy to stop Thor from hurting the birds, but we have to be very careful to watch out for Satan so that he can't hurt us."—V.L.W.

Thank You, God, for Angels

☀ *For he will command his angels concerning you to guard you in all your ways.* Ps. 91:11, NIV.

Zoom! The snowball whizzed right along the part in James's black hair. He snatched the cap out of his coat pocket and pulled it over his ears. "I'll get you, Teddy!" James yelled.

James scooped up a handful of snow. Chasing Teddy, he raced down the apartment stairs and across the vacant lot. The boys ran between and around groups of their playmates. James ducked some snowballs flying between some bigger boys. Then, *zoom! wham!* James's handful of snow found its mark on Teddy's shoulder.

"Ah, you got me!" Teddy yelled. He fell on his stomach and into the snow, and James tumbled into the snow beside him. They rolled in the snow until their dark blue jackets were white. The boys had just agreed to make the biggest snowman on Union Street when the bigger boys began pelting them with snowballs.

"Ouch!" James cried out. "These snowballs are hard!"

Teddy sprang to his feet and scampered toward the apartment building. But James, who was a bit chubby, was not quite as fast. The teenagers cornered him. He felt afraid.

"James! James, come here!" his mother called from across the street.

"Yes, Mother!" James answered.

When the teenagers saw James's mother coming across the street, they ran to the other end of the vacant lot. James galloped toward Mother.

"This story happened to me a long time ago," Dr. James North says. "I was so glad to know that my mother was watching over me. All 8-year-old boys need a mother's care sometimes. And bigger boys need care, too. That's why I'm glad that even when I'm teaching at the Seventh-day Adventist seminary an angel watches over me."

You have your very own angel, too. Aren't you glad?—F.J.C.

Sugar Gets Lost

Ask, and it shall be given you; seek, and ye shall find; knock, and it shall be opened unto you. Matt. 7:7.

Sugar! Here, Sugar!"

Alex cupped his hands around his mouth, calling at the top of his voice. As he called, he walked around the camp where he and Mother and Daddy had stayed in their trailer the night before.

"Come on, Alex. It's time to go now," Mother called.

"Oh, Mommy, we can't go and leave Sugar here alone. I love Sugar. She's the only dog I ever had."

"I know, son," Mother nodded sadly. "But your father must be back to work by noon today, and we have more than 100 miles to go. We'll help you look for Sugar, but if we don't find her soon, we'll have to go home without her."

Calling and whistling, the family searched the camp again, but Sugar could not be found. Alex cried quietly as they pulled out of the campground and headed for home. He was afraid he would never see Sugar again.

Alex was lonely the next few days without Sugar to play with. Every night he prayed that God would send her back.

One day after Alex had gone to school, Mother and Daddy talked about what could be done. They decided that Sugar could not find her way home.

"Let's get Alex another dog like Sugar," Mother said. She knew that Alex would soon have a birthday. "If we get him another dog, maybe he won't be so sad about Sugar."

"I have to go to Frankfort this afternoon," Daddy answered. "I'll see if I can find a dog like Sugar."

Daddy backed his car out of the driveway and headed toward Frankfort. As he watched the road ahead, he noticed a dog running down the road toward him.

As the dog came closer, Daddy thought it looked familiar. Could this dog with the dirty gray fur and thin body be Sugar?

Quickly Daddy put his foot on the brake and stopped by the dog. Before he could call, the dirty bundle of fur, barking and wagging her tail excitedly, ran up to the side of the car. Sure enough, Sugar was on her way home.

When Daddy opened the car door, Sugar jumped into the car. When they arrived home later that afternoon, Alex had come back from school.

"Oh, Sugar! Sugar! I knew that God would answer my prayer." Alex hugged Sugar, dirt and all.

"Well," Daddy said as he smiled at Mother, "we'll not have to get a new dog after all." — M.K.S.

Buffy, Tea, and Prayer

Now My eyes will be open and My ears attentive to prayer made in this place. 2 Chron. 7:15, NKJV.

Mommy, please come and look at Buffy. I don't think she's feeling good."

Buffy was the Thomases' children's dog—a golden retriever. Any other day Buffy would have been running around the house, or if she were outside, she would be chasing birds or other creatures. But not today. Buffy was inside the house, lying on the floor. Buffy was quiet. Buffy was sick.

The children came, knelt down on the floor, and looked at their beloved dog.

"What's the matter with her, Mommy?" asked Donna-Maria.

"I don't know, honey. Perhaps Buffy has eaten some bad food that has made her sick," said Mother.

Mother patted Buffy's head, but Buffy didn't even lift her head. She just lay there. Mother knew something was wrong with Buffy, but what it was she didn't know.

"Mommy, please do something," the children cried.

Mother looked at the children's sad faces, and then she looked at Buffy. In her heart Mother was praying for Jesus to help her.

"I will make a tea for Buffy," said Mother, "and maybe the tea will help her feel better." So Mother made catnip tea and let it cool. Mother started giving the tea to Buffy. One spoonful, then another spoonful of the tea was put into the dog's mouth until all the tea was gone. Then Mother and the children prayed for Buffy. They asked Jesus to please heal their dog.

All morning Buffy slept. When the children walked by the dog, they stopped and patted her, but Buffy never moved—she slept on.

With their dog sick, the Thomas children didn't feel like playing. They were sitting quietly in Clarence's bedroom when they heard a noise. They looked up, and there was Buffy, running into the bedroom. She hopped onto the bed and began playing with the children.

The children jumped up and down, laughing and hugging Buffy. Jesus had healed their dog.

That night at family worship, when Daddy asked the children what they were thankful to Jesus for, they all said the same thing: "I'm thankful that Jesus healed Buffy."—C.B.T.

Waiting for Wings

I said, "I wish I had wings like a dove." Ps. 55:6, ICB.

Mom, I sure wish I could fly," sighed Bea Jay as she watched the pigeons do their flying stunts above the shed.

"I always wanted to fly too," laughed Mom. "When I was a little girl, my brother and I prayed every day for wings so that we could fly up above the clouds—all the way to God's house! Every morning," Mom continued, "my brother would look for wings on my back and say, 'Nope. Nuthin' yet.' And I'd look at his bony little shoulder blades and say, 'I think they are a little bigger today, but I don't see any feathers yet.'

"Oh, we really *believed* God would say yes to our prayers for wings. And I was sure my mother would make my dresses with little holes in the back for my wings!"

Bea Jay giggled at the thought of Mom flying around with wings on her back. "But Mom, you don't have wings yet. Why didn't God answer your prayers?"

"Oh, He *did.* He knew that wings might be more trouble than they were worth—here on earth. And where everyone else has only arms and legs, I'd be a freak!

"It's OK for God to answer any way He thinks is best, you know. Sometimes He answers yes; sometimes He answers no. As for my prayers for wings, God said, 'Wait! Wait until you get to heaven! There everybody will be able to fly!'

"And we will be able to fly around and visit planets—maybe Jupiter and Mars!" said Mom.

"What fun!" exclaimed Bea. "But first, I want to fly to God's house and say 'thank You' to Jesus," said Bea.

"Me too," said Mom.—B.V.

Johnny's Change

☀ *And do not forget to do good and to share with others. Heb. 13:16, NIV.*

"**G**ive me that!" Johnny jerked his car away from Adam. Adam picked up a book to look at.

"That's my book. Put it down."

Sara found a puzzle on the floor to play with.

"That's my puzzle. Give me that!" screamed Johnny.

Soon Sara and Adam left Johnny's house and went to their home. Johnny went to the kitchen to talk to his mother.

"Mom, I don't have anyone to play with."

"Why, what happened to Sara and Adam?" asked Mother.

"They left."

"Oh, is something wrong?"

"Mom, I didn't share my toys and so they left. Now I don't have anyone to play with," Johnny sobbed.

"What do you think could change that, Johnny?"

"I guess if I change and be nice and share my toys."

"Yes, Johnny. Sometimes it is hard to share, but Jesus can help us."

"Can I ask Him now?"

"Sure."

Johnny prayed: "Jesus, thank You for all my toys. Please help me share my toys. Amen."

The next day Sara and Adam came over again to play with Johnny. Sara picked up one of Johnny's favorite books. Johnny almost said "That's mine," but he remembered his prayer. Instead, he said, "You can look in my book. That's my favorite." Sara was happy and Johnny was too.

Do you have trouble sharing sometimes? Remember, Jesus can help you. —E.G.N.

"It Will Be Yours!"

✷ *Whatever you ask for in prayer, believe that you have received it, and it will be yours. Mark 11:24, NIV.*

Did Jesus send the money yet, Mommy?" Marlene asked.

Mother answered gently, "Not yet. But I'm sure He will answer our prayer."

Mother and the children had prayed for Jesus to send the money so that they could get their car fixed.

After Marlene left, Mother said an extra little prayer. "Lord, we do need our car repaired so that we can go to camp meeting. Please help us. Amen."

Then Wayne came rushing into the room. "Everything is itching me, Mommy!" His face looked like a big red strawberry. Mother put calamine lotion on it and decided that she would have to take him in the noisy old car to the doctor.

On the way to the doctor's office, Mother realized that the car wasn't making noise anymore. And by the time they got to the office, Wayne's rash was almost gone.

Later that evening when Daddy took the car to the mechanic, the man said, "It's in perfect condition. What did you do?"

"My family prayed," Daddy said.

And so off they went to camp meeting. After everyone was asleep in the tent that night, Marlene asked in a whisper, "Mommy, do you think Jesus fixed our car and let Wayne get the rash so we could know it was fixed?"

"I'm sure He did," Mommy said.

Jesus hears us when we pray. —A.C.B.

Apple Trees Are Gifts

☀ The way you give to others is the way God will give to you. Luke 6:38, ICB.

Ten-year-old Wintley Phipps smiled at his reflection in the window of the Air Canada plane. "Quite nice!" he said, admiring the gray derby that matched his suit. "My very first suit," he sighed.

Taking off his derby, Wintley leaned forward to examine the seat belt for the hundredth time. He would have plenty of time to figure out how the seat belt was made. He was flying from Trinidad to Barbados to Antigua to Bermuda and finally to Canada.

"I will enjoy every minute of inspecting the seat belts," Wintley said to his brother Wendell.

"Me too," Wendell said, munching the mints the stewardess had given to him.

"Thank you," Wintley told the stewardess. He leaned back in his seat. Between bites, he said, "Wendell, we'll be able to see more and do much more in Canada than we could on our small island. And there will be apple trees!"

"Yes, Wintley. I'm sure that God has planned many wonderful gifts for you boys in Montreal." Mrs. Phipps spoke softly from across the aisle.

Wintley yawned. "Mother's voice sounds like bubbles," Wintley told Wendell. "Bubbles that pop softly in the hot sun." Wintley snuggled back in the soft pillows of the seat. *Many wonderful new gifts,* Wintley said to himself again and again. He imagined soft blue bubbles, the color of Mother's dress, as he began to fall asleep. The bubbles seemed to pop, pop, pop, spraying his nose with water.

"We're here!" Wendell shrieked.

"What? What?" Wintley asked, rubbing his eyes. He tried to jump up to look around, but the seat belt held him fast.

After what seemed like a long time, Wintley followed his parents down the ramp of the airplane. "Come, Wendell!" Wintley said, tugging on Wendell's jacket. "God has many wonderful new gifts waiting for us!"

Today Pastor Wintley Phipps lives in Columbia, Maryland. He writes and sings many songs about the wonderful gifts God gives us. One song says, "Lord, You've given me more than I could think of, . . . more than I could dream of. Lord, You've given me Your all . . . ; I give You my life."

What is the best gift you have ever received? What is the best gift you can give to Jesus?—F.J.C.

Waiting

When everything is ready, then I will come and get you, so that you can always be with me. John 14:3, TLB.

Jerry hurried to the school bus. His faithful dog, Jonah, trotted beside him. "You'd better go home now," Jerry told Jonah when they reached the bus stop. But Jonah didn't go back. He waited until the bus came and took Jerry away. The bus turned a corner and disappeared. Still Jonah didn't go home.

The dog waited all morning. He watched down the road.

At noon Jonah must have been hungry, but he didn't go home for lunch. He waited for Jerry to come back. After a while it got colder, then it started snowing, but Jonah didn't go home. He waited for Jerry to come back. The wind came up, and it snowed harder. Jonah didn't budge from the spot where Jerry had left him.

Finally, after a long, long day filled with cold and wind and snow, the big yellow school bus came around the corner and stopped. A moment later Jerry ran down the steps and hugged his faithful dog.

Did you know that one day soon Jesus is coming back too? He's coming to take you and me to heaven to be with Him forever. Are you waiting and watching for Him, as Jonah watched for Jerry? Jesus will be so happy if you do. And so will you. —V.L.W.

The Selfish Birthday Girl

When you do things, do not let selfishness . . . be your guide.
Phil. 2:3, ICB.

Julie was angry when Shannon won the prize. "I wanted to win
that!" she shouted. Julie had hoped to win the beautiful barrette
ever since Mommy had bought it for a prize at her birthday party.

Julie stomped her foot and ran off to her room. Everyone watched
in surprise. "I don't want to!" she cried when Mommy tried to encour-
age her to be nice and come back to play another game with her
friends.

Julie wouldn't even come out to tell her friends goodbye as they
left the party.

"Why is my girl acting so naughty?" Daddy asked as he sat by Julie
on the bed. Julie didn't answer.

Daddy sat by Julie for a long time. "Did you have a good time
today, Julie?" he finally asked.

At first Julie was angry. "No, I didn't," she answered. "I thought
this would be the best day ever. Why was it so bad?"

"Who were you thinking about all the time?" Daddy asked.

Julie was quiet for a long time before she understood what was
wrong. "I was thinking about me," she whispered. "And I thought
about all the presents and winning prizes. I was mad when my friends
won the games." Julie started to cry. Daddy pulled her onto his lap. "I
really didn't mean to be so selfish," she said.

"It's hard to feel good when you just think about yourself. Jesus
made us to care about other people," Daddy said. "Let's talk to Him
about how you feel and what happened today."

"I think that will help." Julie gave a little smile.

They knelt by Julie's bed together. The words were hard at first,
then easier as Julie knew that Jesus was listening. "I don't like how I
acted today," Julie prayed. "It ruined my whole party. Please forgive
me. Amen."

Julie felt new again. Daddy smiled and asked, "Is there a happy
6-year-old birthday girl here again?"

"Yes! I want to start over, even if my friends aren't here. Can we try the box game again?" Julie asked.

"I want to play too!" Mommy called from the doorway.

"I'm going to have another birthday party today," Julie giggled. "I'm so glad Jesus lets us start over new." —L.R.

A Cheerful Heart

✳ *A cheerful heart is good medicine. Prov. 17:22, NIV.*

I promised you that I would patch your doll, Ketai, when I got some glue," Mommy said.

"I want to take her to bed with me, but her face is broken." Ketai was unhappy that she had dropped her new doll with the pretty brown face, and now there was a big crack across dolly's forehead. Ketai had cried and cried, and now she had a fever.

"You must stop crying, Ketai, or your fever will get worse, and you'll have to take more medicine."

"I want to stop crying, but every time I think of my beautiful doll I get sad again."

"Well," Mommy said, "do you think crying will help?"

"No, ma'am," Ketai said as she tried to wipe away her tears.

Then Mommy had a good idea. "Ketai, remember your memory verse, the one about good medicine?"

"Yes, Mommy. It says 'A cheerful heart is good medicine.' "

"Right! So let's do something cheerful. How about planning your birthday party? That should make you feel better."

After a while Ketai said with a big smile, "I'm happy now, Mommy, and I feel better. I'm glad I didn't have to take any more real medicine."

Can you think of a time when you needed good medicine?— A.C.B.

Saved From Death

For the Son of Man has come to save that which was lost. Matt. 18:11, NKJV.

Meow, meow," came the soft, tiny voice calling out from the city dump. Anna and Kate looked down and discovered a pitiful little kitten—hungry, scraggly, and bleeding. It was crying for help. The two women felt sorry for him. So off he went to Anna and Kate's house. They prayed for the poor little kitten. "Dear Jesus, don't let Deemed die." They named him Deemed because he was redeemed, or saved, from death.

With tender loving care and plenty of warm goat's milk, pretty soon Deemed grew to be a beautiful cat with long, pretty fur.

Every evening Anna and Kate would hold meetings to tell people about Jesus. They painted a sign with big white letters, "Want a Friend? Come to Jesus," and put it in their window. Many people read the sign and came to hear about Jesus. One day Anna and Kate said, "Let's take Deemed to the mission tonight. Let's tell the people what Jesus did for a poor little kitten. Maybe they will see what Jesus can do for them."

So that night Deemed went to the mission. They held him up and told the people what Jesus had done for Deemed. Then they told the people that just as Deemed had been saved from dying in the dump, Jesus wanted to save *them* and take *them* to heaven. Many people decided that they wanted to go to heaven with Jesus.

Jesus came down to the "dump" of this world and found all of us lost and dying. He wants to help us get ready to go to heaven. Do you want to go to heaven? I do! I hope you do, too.—P.H.

Helping Mr. Duck

Then God saw everything that He had made, and indeed it was very good. Gen. 1:31, NKJV.

Five-year-old Danny loved to feed the ducks in the city park. When the ducks saw Danny carrying a bag of Mother's whole-wheat bread they would waddle toward him as fast as they could, quacking loudly. They loved to eat Mother's bread.

One day Danny sat on a bench as he watched the ducks swim in the lake. One duck dipped his head under the water to look for a nice fat tadpole to eat. Suddenly he jerked his head up out of the water. Danny could see that a piece of floating plastic had gotten caught on the duck's beak. The duck shook his head, trying to get the plastic off, but it would not come off. The plastic only wrapped itself tighter. The poor duck could not open his beak to eat or drink.

"Come here, Mr. Duck," Danny called. "I'll take the plastic off your beak." But of course Mr. Duck didn't understand. He swam away, still shaking his head.

Danny ran to the park attendant and told him about the duck. "I will try to catch him," the attendant told Danny. But the frightened duck did not know that people only wanted to help him. He swam farther away to the middle of the lake. Many days passed before someone was able to catch Mr. Duck and take the plastic off his beak. Mr. Duck was glad to be able to eat again.

God wants us to take care of the beautiful world and the animals that He has made. You can help by always throwing paper trash and other litter into the garbage can, where it belongs. The animals do not want it in their homes, either!

What other things can you do to help take care of God's world?— C.B.E.

Having Fun Anyway!

☀️ *This is the day which the Lord has made; we will rejoice and be glad in it. Ps. 118:24, NKJV.*

Ashley pressed her nose against the window glass. She felt tingly and excited inside as she watched Uncle Warren and Aunt Betty's car pull to a stop in the driveway. Big sister, Heather, went running out the door to greet cousins Mark and Jennifer. Ashley was only 4 and feeling a little shy, since her cousins were older.

"We brought our skates," Ashley heard 12-year-old Mark call. "Want to skate, Heather?"

"Sure, that will be fun!" answered Heather, running off to get her skates.

"I can skate, too!" Ashley said softly.

"Sure you can, Two Pint. Come here and give me a hug," Jennifer responded. The cousins all went to get their skates.

Ashley slowly made her way down the driveway to the sidewalk, where the big kids waited. "Hurry up, Ashley," sister Heather shouted.

"Follow the leader, and I'm it," commanded Mark. Off the big kids flew, but Ashley couldn't keep up.

With tears running down her cheeks, Ashley sat down and took off her skates. Up to the house she went with her skates banging against her legs. No fun today, because she couldn't play with the big kids. Ashley felt pretty lonesome and sad inside.

"Ashley . . . Ashley . . ." Was that Aunt Betty calling?

Quickly Ashley ran through the front door into the kitchen.

"Ashley, would you like to help us make a pie?" Aunt Betty asked.

Nodding her head up and down, Ashley climbed up on the stool by the kitchen deck. Maybe she would have fun today even without the big kids! —P.M.M.

God Works for Good

We know that in all things God works for good with those who love him. Rom. 8:28, TEV.

Tommy frowned. He felt real sad. His best friend, Peter, was going to move away.

"Peter's all upset," Tommy said to his daddy as the two of them raked leaves in the yard. "He doesn't want to live somewhere else. He likes it in Allentown." Tommy swallowed hard. "I don't want him to move. We're friends."

Dad raked some more leaves. "I know. I was talking to Peter's dad the other day. He doesn't want to leave here, either. But he has to have a job."

Tommy kept raking. "But why did he lose his job here? Why did God let that happen?"

"We don't know, son. Things happen that we can't understand."

Tommy thought some more. "What if *you* have to get a new job?"

Dad shook his head. "I don't think that's going to happen. But if it did, we'd manage. You see, sometimes we don't understand God's ways. But we can still be sure that everything will work out for the best, because we love God and we belong to Him and He loves us."

"But things don't always seem to work," Tommy said.

Dad nodded. "I know, son. But we have to go on believing in God." He looked at his watch. "We've raked enough leaves for today. Why don't you go play with Peter for a while? And tell him that as soon as they get settled in their new place we want him to come to visit you."

Tommy smiled. He felt better already. He put the rake carefully against a tree. "Thanks, Dad. I'll help you finish the leaves tomorrow." And he hurried off to tell Peter the good news about the visit. —N.C.P.

"Give Me a Bible"

And I say to you, ask, and it will be given to you. Luke 11:9, NKJV.

The man was standing in the living room. The woman who lived in the house saw him as she was leaving the bedroom and going into the kitchen. It scared her to see a strange man in her house; no one had told him to come into her house.

"Who are you?" the woman asked. "What do you want? Who told you to come inside my house?" The man didn't answer the woman. He just stood there with his hands at his sides as he looked at the bookcase in the living room. The woman asked again, "Who are you? What do you want?" The man kept staring at the bookcase on the living-room wall. The bookcase was filled with many books. Why was this man looking so hard at the books in the bookcase? What did he want?

The man pointed to the bookcase and said in the Portuguese language, "Give me a Bible, please." The woman answered in Portuguese, "A Bible? The only Bible I have is in English. Do you speak English?" The man did not speak English. The man said again in Portuguese, "Give me a Bible, please."

The woman walked over to the bookcase. She looked at the many books. She found the Bible and took it off the shelf. She turned and gave the Bible to the man. A big smile came on the man's face as he took the Bible from the woman's hand. *"Obrigado, obrigado* [thank you, thank you]," said the man over and over again as he held the Bible in his hands. He looked at the Bible and rubbed his hands over it.

The woman smiled and said, "You're welcome."

The man turned from the woman and walked out the front door of the house. The woman never saw the man again. But Jesus knows who that man is and where that man is living. Jesus also knows why that man asked for the Bible. —C.B.T.

Big Brother

✹ *Remember the Sabbath day by keeping it holy. Ex. 20:8, NIV.*

Jimmy was happy about Jerry, his new "Big Brother"! He had no brothers or sisters and looked forward to each visit from Jerry.

It was Sabbath afternoon, and Jimmy was sitting on the porch and playing a Bible game. It was so hot that he wondered if he might be able to roast marshmallows on the sidewalk.

Then he looked up and saw Jerry. "Hi, sport, ready for a trip to the park?" Jerry asked.

"Yep! Sure am! Let me go tell Daddy. What're we gonna do?"

"Hold on!" Jerry said. "Let's get there first."

Jimmy stopped on his way up the steps. "But I need to know what we're gonna do."

"We're going to play ball," Jerry said, "and buy some good old popcorn and lemonade. Then go to the fun house."

Oops! Jimmy thought. *It's Sabbath. What can I tell Jerry?* Then with a determined look on his little face he said, "Jerry, I don't play ball or buy things on the Sabbath."

"The Sabbath," Jerry said, looking puzzled. "Why not?"

"Because Jesus wants us to keep the Sabbath holy."

"Well, suppose you tell me about it on the way to the park. How about a nature hike?"

"That's good!" Jimmy said with a grown-up look. "That's good!"

Jesus is always happy when we obey Him. —A.C.B.

Like a Lion

Be alert, be on the watch! Your enemy, the Devil, roams around like a roaring lion, looking for someone to devour. 1 Peter 5:8, TEV.

Near our camp in South Africa's largest game park was a river. As we drove toward the bridge that crossed the river we saw several huge cats climb up the bank and onto the road. They were lions. We watched as another lion and another came up from the river. We counted 14 African lions. Driving slowly, we followed them. When they got to the bridge several stopped, sat down, and looked at us. From our car window they seemed tame. Their beautiful brown eyes looked kind. Finally, they crossed the bridge and disappeared into the bushes on the other side.

"Didn't they look friendly as they wagged the black tuft of hair on the end of their tails?" I said. "It would be fun to pet one."

But a little later that day I changed my mind. By the roadside we saw four lions eating a buffalo they had just killed. Watching from our car window, I heard their growls. I saw their sharp claws rip open the tough hide, and I saw their teeth tear the flesh as they ate the meat. Now I understood that each lion in that game park was looking for something to kill and eat.

Like the devil, the lions looked harmless as they sat on the bridge. But if I had left our car and walked toward them, they might have chosen to eat me!

Jesus says, "Watch out for the devil." He's like those lions. He makes you think it's all right to hit your playmate, take something that is not yours, or disobey your mother. But he's really keeping you from being ready to meet Jesus when He comes. Ask Jesus to help you not to be fooled by the devil. —E.E.L.

It's OK to Be Different

Man looketh on the outward appearance, but the Lord looketh on the heart. 1 Sam. 16:7.

What big eggs these are!" exclaimed Joyce.

"They're duck eggs," said Uncle Wilson, handing them to her. "If we put them in Cluck-Cluck's nest, she will hatch some ducklings for us along with her chicks."

In about three weeks the eggs began to crack open, and out popped a dozen fuzzy, little yellow chicks—and three yellow ducklings. "Feed me, feed me!" they all cheeped at once!

"Cluck, cluck, cluck," said their mother. "Follow me. Watch me."

She taught them how to scratch for worms and bugs to eat and how to hide under her wings when they were in danger. She didn't notice that some of her babies were different from the other chicks. She loved them all. And she tried every day to teach them what all good chickens should know.

One day it rained very hard, and the creek came up into the yard! The frightened chicks ran quickly under their mother's wings—except the ones that were "different." Those baby ducks played happily in the creek. Mother Cluck-Cluck was frantic. "Cluck, cluck, squawk, squawk, SQUAWK!" she screamed. "Come back! Don't you know that chicks can't swim!" But the fluffy ducklings bobbed merrily, and safely, on top the water—just like ducks are supposed to do, *because God made them that way!*

Poor Mother Cluck-Cluck didn't know that God made chickens different than ducks. She was doing what she thought she should. And the ducks were doing what they thought they should.

God made all kinds of children, too—each one is different from the other. He loves them all—just the way they are. And we should too.—B.V.

"Is That Me?"

The Lord does not look at the things man looks at. 1 Sam. 16:7, NIV.

Skip danced along the pavement beside his big brother Dane. "Won't we ever get there?" he asked as he tugged on Dale's jacket sleeve. "You're the best brother in the whole world."

Dale grinned down at Skip. "You're just saying that because I'm taking you to the amusement park."

"That's not the only reason," Skip protested. He smiled and showed off the gap where his first baby tooth had come out. "But I'm really glad we get to go."

"Me too." Dale lowered his voice. "I wouldn't let the guys I hang out with know it, but I'll never get over being a kid when it comes to fun."

"Good." Skip speeded up to match his brother's longer steps.

The amusement park proved to be everything and more than Skip had hoped. All kinds of games and crazy rides, buttered popcorn and cotton candy. "We don't usually stuff our faces with junk food like cotton candy," Dale warned his little brother. "But just this once we'll have some." He bought balloons for them both.

"Is that everything?" Skip finally asked.

"Not quite." Dale led Skip to a wall of mirrors. "Look."

"Is that *me?*" Skip cried. One mirror made him fat. Another made him skinny. One made him tall, another short. The brothers had fun looking into the crazy mirrors.

Aren't you glad God looks at our hearts instead of our not-so-perfect faces and bodies? —C.L.R.

The Man and the Milk

For your Father knows the things you have need of before you ask Him. Matt. 6:8, NKJV.

B.G.'s hungry stomach led him right to the refrigerator. He yanked open the door, and finding it empty, he exclaimed, "When are we going to get some milk?"

Neither B.G.'s mom nor dad had a job, so there was no money to buy food or milk.

"Guess we'll need to have a visit from the raven," his dad said.

Do you know the story of Elijah and how God sent the raven to feed him? Well, B.G. knew that story too and accepted that answer. He closed the refrigerator door and skipped out the door to school. B.G.'s dad went to his class, where he was studying to be a pastor. After class a man walked up to B.G.'s daddy and asked, "Can you use some milk?"

B.G.'s dad laughed and said, "We sure could."

The man said, "I'll bring some over." And he did.

That afternoon B.G. came from school, opened the refrigerator door, and shouted, "Where did this milk come from?"

"We had a visit from the raven," his dad said, smiling.

We know that it was really a man who brought the milk, don't we? How do you think that man knew that B.G.'s daddy needed some milk? If you said God helped him know, you are right. —E.G.N.

Milk and More

God shall supply all your needs. Phil. 4:19, NASB.

B.G.'s family still didn't have food to eat. Even though his mom and dad continued to look for jobs, they hadn't found any.

The next day B.G. was thankful that he had milk to drink, but his little stomach ached for more food. He left for school as usual.

B.G.'s dad didn't have class that morning, so B.G.'s mom and dad continued their morning worship long after B.G. left. B.G.'s dad played the piano and his mother sang praises to Jesus. Music filled the small apartment when suddenly it was interrupted by one loud knock at the door. The door wasn't far from the piano, and B.G.'s mother, wondering who it might be, ran immediately to the door.

B.G.'s mother opened the door, looked to her left, then to her right. She looked out, but she saw no one. Then she looked down, and there in front of the door were two large bags full of the groceries they needed.

God said He will provide all your needs. Trust Him. —E.G.N.

The Difference

A happy heart is like good medicine. Prov. 17:22, ICB.

Imani (Ee-MON-ee) and Nakia (Nah-KEE-ya) are neighbors. They have lived next door to each other all their lives, and they even look a lot alike. During the week both wear their black hair in cornrows, with a curl in front—right in the middle of the forehead. For Sabbath school their mothers brush their hair out into soft waves that fall to their shoulders and tie a ribbon on the curl. Both have what Imani's daddy calls "brown button noses," and both are missing two front teeth.

But their neighbor, Mr. Monroe, says there is one way that they are not alike. "I usually hear those little girls before I see them," Mr. Monroe told his wife and chuckled. "And I can always tell which one I hear before I see her," he added. "Imani has a cheerful sound to her voice even when she isn't singing. And she does a lot of singing and humming. But Nakia," he said, shaking his head sadly, "is usually yelling 'Why?' or 'What!' or 'Make me!' or whining. Her noise and complaining actually give me a headache sometimes. Wife," he wondered out loud while rubbing his chin, "I just don't know what makes them behave so differently! They both have nice parents and lovely homes."

Do you have any idea what makes Imani so cheerful or Nakia so unpleasant? See if you can find a clue in the Bible text above.

Can you think of three ways to keep your heart happy?

Two clues: Psalm 9:2; 147:1, 3. —F.J.C.

Joy

(Xandi's Song)

Words and Music by
Faith Johnson Crumbly

2) I can sing in the rain and smile on a cloudy day.
I know the sun will shine again for me.
And like the rainbow that spans the sky,
My joy spreads far and wide for all to see.

68

Can Jesus Really Hear Us?

You know when I sit and when I rise. Ps. 139:2, NIV.

"D addy," Wayne said, "can God hear us way up in heaven? I was saying my prayers and wondered if He could hear me."

"Yes, son," Daddy answered. "God can *always* hear us."

"All the time?" Wayne asked.

"Yes, because He's always with us. Three special words describe God. The first is 'omnipresent.' Say it after me slowly—om-ni-pres-ent."

"Om-ni-pres-ent," Wayne said slowly.

"The first part—'omni'—means all. Omnipresent means that God is always present. He is always with us, even though we can't see Him.

"The other word, 'omniscient,' means that God is all-wise. Say it slowly, om-nis-ci-ent.

"Wayne," Father continued, "God knows everything in the whole world. So when we pray, He knows what we need, because He knows everything!"

"Wow, Dad!" Wayne said excitedly. "You mean I don't always have to say my prayers out loud because He can always hear and already knows what I need?"

"Yes," Father said. "And the third word, 'om-nip-o-tent,' means that God has all power. So He is always present, always wise, and always powerful."

"That's awesome!" Wayne said. "Thanks a lot, Dad!"—A.C.B.

Almost a Bad Day

☀ *I will teach you what is good and right. 1 Sam. 12:23, ICB.*

Going to school was going to be wonderful! At registration Davy had stood in line and had met a new friend, Joshua.

But now everything was horrible. Davy had been thinking about school as he played with his skateboard. Maybe that is why he had forgotten to be careful.

Maybe I'll try something new, Davy thought. *I'll put one knee on the board and push with my other foot. I'll hang on to the front of the skateboard and go fast a long way down the sidewalk.*

It worked pretty well until he gave a really big push with his left leg. The front of the skateboard caught in a crack. Davy fell forward and felt his face scrape along the rough concrete.

"Mommy, Mommy!" he cried, holding his face as he ran toward the house. "Help, Mommy! My face is hurt!"

Mommy pulled Davy onto her lap and placed a cool bag over the biggest bump on his forehead. "Your face is really scratched, and it's swollen, but it will be a little better in the morning."

Daddy looked at Davy's face. "I'm glad it wasn't any worse."

"Daddy, don't make me go to school tomorrow," Davy pleaded.

"Let's talk about it some more after supper," Daddy suggested.

At worship Davy asked, "What about tomorrow? The kids won't like me. They'll think I'm strange and scary."

They all knelt and Daddy prayed. "Please help Davy in school tomorrow. Help the other students see what a nice person Davy is even if he has scratches on his face. Amen."

Daddy walked Davy to school. They went up to Mrs. Hasel's desk and told her what had happened.

Joshua was the first one to sit down next to Davy. "What happened?" he asked. "Does it hurt?"

Mrs. Hasel helped introduce the students to each other. She helped Davy explain about the bruises and scrapes on his face. Davy was scared at first, but it helped when one of the girls said, "You were really brave to come to school today."

Davy smiled until the scrape on his left cheek started to pull a little. School wasn't going to be so bad after all.

At recess the boys talked to Davy about his skateboard. "I won't ride on my hands and knees anymore," Tommy said.

"I won't either," Davy laughed. "Sidewalks are hard on faces." — L.R.

Can You Imagine?

No eye has seen, no ear has heard . . . what God has prepared for those who love him. 1 Cor. 2:9, NIV.

Can you imagine a conversation between God and Adam and Eve in the very beginning? God said, "Adam and Eve, I want you to have many children, and I want you to rule over all the earth and over all the animals. You can eat any of the fruit in the whole garden except that special tree in the middle."

Adam might have said, "Thank You, Father, for the privilege."

And Eve might have said, "Yes, dear Father, we thank You for creating us and for such great privileges. We will do as You say."

But they didn't always do as God said, and so they lost many privileges. They had to leave their beautiful garden home. And the animals didn't obey them anymore, and Adam and Eve had to work hard for food.

But God forgave them, and He forgives us also when we are disobedient. Let's remember to pray and thank Him for His blessings.

Jesus promises that He is preparing an especially beautiful place for all of us who love Him. He says that place will be better than anything we've ever seen. Do you want to go to that place in heaven?—A.C.B.

The Rainy Day

He veils the sky in clouds and provides rain for the earth; he clothes the hills with grass. Ps. 147:8, REB.

Erica was playing house. Suddenly Grandma heard her say, "I *hate* the rain."

"Is that so?" Grandma asked.

"Yes." Erica's voice was sad.

"Come here, Erica," Grandma beckoned. Erica went to her.

"Do you hate the apples from my apple tree?"

"Of course not," Erica said. "I *love* the apples from your apple tree. And I like the tree, too, because I can climb it."

Grandma asked, "Do you like daffodils, dandelions, and buttercups?"

"I *love* those flowers, Grandma, because they're all yellow, and yellow is my favorite color."

Grandma asked, "Do you like wading in the creek to find minnows and crayfish and pollywogs?"

"Grandma, you know the creek is my favorite place," Erica answered. Then she frowned. "But I can't go there today because of this yucky old rain."

"Well," Grandma sighed, "if there weren't any rain, there wouldn't be any apple trees or apples. All the flowers would die of thirst, and there wouldn't be any animals in the creeks, because there wouldn't even be creeks."

"Oh," Erica said. She was deep in thought as she looked out the streaked, speckled window. The world looked different somehow.

Grandma went into the kitchen to make lunch.

As Erica stirred her steamy soup she said, "I love the rain."

"Is that so?" Grandma was smiling.

"Yes!" Erica said in a happy voice. —V.L.K.

The Vegetable Man

☼ Let the little children come to Me, and do not forbid them; for of such is the kingdom of God. Luke 18:16, NKJV.

When the vegetable man's truck, loaded with lots of bananas, apples, sweet potatoes, candy, and gum, would stop in front of the houses on the street, the children would run out to the truck and shout, "The vegetable man is here! The vegetable man is here!" And the mothers would come out of their houses to see what good things they could buy from him.

The children loved the vegetable man. While the parents were trying to make up their minds what to buy, the children crowded around the vegetable man, asking him questions about his truck, his family, or talking to him about their family and friends. The vegetable man was always patient and kind to the children. He'd let them climb on the truck, or sometimes sit on his lap.

That's the way it was when Jesus lived here on this earth. When Jesus walked into a city all the children would run out to meet Him, grabbing at His hands, walking close to Him, calling out to their mothers, "Jesus is here! Jesus is here!" They would ask Jesus questions about His family and His friends. Jesus loved the children.

When the parents brought their children to Jesus for Him to bless them, Jesus' disciples got mad. They didn't want to bother Jesus with the children, and they tried to keep the children away from Him. But Jesus told His disciples to let the children come. And the children ran to Jesus. Some sat on His lap, others leaned against Him, and some sat on the ground and looked up at Him. And the parents brought their babies to Jesus also, and He blessed them all.

One day Jesus will come back to earth, and He'll be looking for His friends. His friends are those who are obedient, kind, and nice to everyone. And all His friends will be happy to see Him. —C.B.T.

The Pretend Pilgrim

✸Children, obey your parents in all things. Col. 3:20, ICB.

Adam found a little matchbox on the floor of the elevator. It was just the right size to hold his dead June bug. He picked up the box and put it in his pocket.

"Did you have fun at preschool and day care today?" his mother asked as they rode up to the fifth floor.

"We got to color this." Adam held up his picture of Pilgrims outside cooking dinner over an open fire. "Mrs. Lewis says Thanksgiving is a day when everybody is thankful for something. What are we thankful for?" he asked as they left the elevator.

"Nothing," Mother said, opening the door to their apartment. "Hang up your coat while I start dinner."

Adam took the little box out of his pocket before he hung up his coat. There were little wooden matches inside. Just like the ones Grandpa used to light the fire in his fireplace.

"I'm a Pilgrim making Thanksgiving dinner," Adam said in his pretend voice. He crumpled up some paper and piled Lincoln Logs on top. Then he got out a match. Mother had told him never to play with matches. But these were play matches. Adam scraped the match across the side of the box.

A bright flame flared up. Startled, Adam dropped the match. It landed in the crumpled paper and began to burn. Fast.

"Mommy!" Adam yelled.

"What's wrong? Oh!" She threw her dish towel over the flames and stomped out the fire. "Adam, I've told you not to play with matches!" she scolded.

"They were only baby ones," Adam sobbed. "I didn't know they were real."

Adam could feel her shaking as she held him tight. "I was wrong about Thanksgiving," she said. "We do have something to be thankful for. You're safe, and we still have each other."—M.H.D.

They Followed a Porpoise

*☀ He leads the humble in the right way and teaches them his will.
Ps. 25:9, TEV.*

You would love the friendly animals called porpoises that swim
in the ocean. They like to play and leap out of the water.
Hidden rocks do not bother them because they can swim
around the rocks safely.

But sailors who sail in ships cannot see the rocks under the water.
Sometimes the ships hit the hidden rocks and sink to the bottom of the
ocean. A long time ago a ship was sailing in a place called Pelorus
Sound, where many sharp rocks were under the water out of sight. The
sailors were afraid because the wind blew hard and the waves were
high. Then they saw a porpoise leap out of the water.

"Let's follow that porpoise," said one sailor. "He's lived here all
his life and knows the way."

"No," said the captain. "He's only a porpoise, and I am captain of
this ship."

"Please, sir, follow him. He knows a lot more about Pelorus Sound
than we do. He could save our lives and lead us around the rocks we
can't see." So the captain put aside his pride, and he followed the
porpoise, which led them safely through the rocks.

From then on, sailors always watched for the porpoise they called
Pelorus Jack. When they tooted their horn, the porpoise leaped up.
They gave him a cheer, and followed him. For 40 years Pelorus Jack
guided many ships through the rocks in those dangerous waters. Not
one ship was lost. Many lives were saved because the sailors humbly
followed the porpoise that knew the way.

Sometimes boys and girls want to go their own way. They don't
want to hold Mother's hand when they cross the street. They think
they can go by themselves. But if they will do what Mother says and
follow her, like the captain who followed the porpoise, they will be
safe and much happier. —E.E.L.

Stuck in a Bucket

No good thing does the Lord withhold from those who walk uprightly. Ps. 84:11, RSV.

Little Brother was wearing his pretty white suit when Mother noticed that he had a piece of chocolate candy melting in each hand—and much of the chocolate was on his face! Mother quickly grabbed a wet washcloth and rushed to wipe away the mess.

When Little Brother saw her coming, he thought she was going to take away his candy, and he wanted to keep his candy! "No, *no*, NO!" he cried. And he backed away as fast as his little legs could go.

Mother hurried to catch up with him. "Wait! Wait! Stop!" she ordered, but Little Brother did not stop. He backed all the way into the corner of the kitchen—right into a large pail full of dirty dishwater and garbage!

What a sorry sight! He was stuck in that nasty bucket. His little arms and legs stuck up out of the dirty water, garbage was squishing all around him, and tears were making stripes in the chocolate on his face, but he still held on to the precious candy!

"Oh, dear, dear, *dear!*" cried Mother as she pulled him out of the bucket and took off the ruined suit. She washed away the tears and the melted candy.

Hugging him as he sobbed on her shoulder, she said, "Honey, I didn't want to take away your candy. I just wanted to keep you clean. *I love you!*"

God loves us, too. And He does not want to take away any good thing from us. He just wants to keep our hearts clean. —B.V.

Burdens

✴ *Help carry one another's burdens, and in this way you will obey the law of Christ. Gal. 6:2, TEV.*

Billy smiled. He liked going to the grocery store with Daddy. They bought different things to eat.

Billy pulled on Daddy's sleeve. "Let's go look at the fruit," he said. "Maybe we'll find something new."

Daddy smiled. "You mean like the kiwis we bought last week?"

Billy laughed. "Yes! Mom was surprised to see them."

Billy pushed the cart toward the fruit section of the store. There were the kiwis, neatly piled up. An old lady was standing there looking at them.

"They're very good—" Billy started to tell her.

But the old lady jumped and bumped the pile of fruit. Kiwis rolled off the counter and all over the floor. It was funny to see kiwis rolling all around. Billy started to laugh. But then he looked at Daddy. Daddy was frowning. " 'Help carry one another's burdens,' " Daddy said.

But, Billy thought, the old lady wasn't carrying anything. She was looking down at the floor and at the kiwis scattered all around. She looked awfully sad.

Then Billy got an idea. If he picked up the kiwis, the old lady wouldn't have to do it. "I'll get them," he said. He handed them to her, and she piled them back up on the counter. When he found the last one and stood up, she was smiling at him.

"I'm sorry I scared you," Billy said. "I just wanted to tell you that kiwis taste good. We bought some last week."

"I think I'll take some home and try them," the old lady said. "And while I'm eating them I'll think about the nice boy who helped me."

Daddy and Billy got the rest of their groceries. On the way home Billy asked, "Is that what it means, Daddy, to carry one another's burdens? It means helping people?"

Daddy nodded. "That's right, Billy. That's what it means."—N.C.P.

Raggedy Ann

☀Your law is my delight. Ps. 119:77, NKJV.

Raggedy Ann came prancing happily into the hospital laundry where two ladies worked. No, Raggedy Ann was not a doll. She was a beautiful dog whose bushy tail wagged merrily about. But not for long. Suddenly the two ladies heard a loud screeching, "Yelp! Yelp! Yelp!"

They looked over to discover that Raggedy Ann's beautiful tail had been caught in the powerful fan behind a machine. One of the boys quickly ran to shut off the motor. Raggedy Ann came whimpering to her master. Her mangled tail wasn't pretty anymore. And Raggedy Ann wasn't prancing about as she had been. Instead of wagging, her tail lay limp between her legs.

One lady said to the other, "I don't think Raggedy Ann will ever want to come here again."

The next week Raggedy Ann *did* come back, still prancing merrily about. But this time something was different. She was on a leash!

Raggedy Ann's master realized that in order to protect her from danger he must place the dog on a leash. The man didn't do it because he wanted to keep her from being happy. He knew that the leash was for Raggedy Ann's own good. And Raggedy Ann seemed just as happy—maybe even happier—on the leash.

God's holy law is kind of like a leash—a leash of love to keep us from doing things that would hurt us, hurt others, and hurt God, and so keep us out of heaven! Isn't God wonderful? He gave us His laws for our own good and happiness!—P.H.

A Lesson From the Birds

Look at the birds. They don't plant or harvest. They don't save food in houses or barns. But God takes care of them. And you are worth much more than birds. Luke 12:24, ICB.

Lynn and her mother stood on the balcony of their apartment. They were watching some small brown birds eat at the bird feeder hanging in a small maple tree. Their neighbor Mrs. Moses had hung the red feeder last year and kept it filled with birdseed all year long.

"Look how the birds take turns eating in Mrs. Moses' birdie restaurant," Lynn whispered to her mother. Several small wrens perched on branches around the feeder. As a bird left one of the feeder windows, another took its place.

"There's no pushing," Lynn whispered.

"And no angry bird words," Mother said.

They both giggled softly.

"Oh, no!" Lynn shouted, pointing to two large gray pigeons swooping toward the bird feeder. But the birds quickly turned and landed under the tree. They began eating seeds that had fallen there.

"Goodie!" Lynn clapped her hands. "They're not pushy birds."

"These birds seem to know that God has provided food for all of them," Mother said. "Mrs. Moses is God's helper."

How do you know that God cares for _____ [child's name]?

What are the names of some of God's helpers who care for you?— F.J.C.

"Come Unto Me"

Come unto me. Matt. 11:28.

Mother, what does Jesus mean when He says, 'Come unto Me'?" Ketai asked.

Ketai was a nice, quiet little girl who was very helpful. She often asked serious questions. So Mother was not surprised at this one.

Mother thought for a while and said a little prayer. "Well, Ketai, when Jesus says 'Come unto Me,' He means that we should come to Him in prayer. Like when you kneel down to pray at night. 'Come unto Me' is a special invitation to tell Him about how you're feeling. It's Jesus' way to invite you to come to Him when you need help—if you're afraid, or if you can't go to sleep at night, or whenever you need help. Do you understand, sweetie?"

"I think so, Mommy," Ketai said. "Like I know I can come to you when I'm hungry and you give me dinner or an apple or something?"

"Yes," Mommy said, "that's what I mean! And remember, Jesus is always ready to answer your prayers."

"Thanks, Mommy," Ketai said. "Now I can tell my friend Billy, 'cause he wants to know what 'come unto Me' means too. We thought we were supposed to go to heaven, and we sure didn't know how to do that."

Jesus always wants us to come to Him. —A.C.B.

Growing Like a Tree

He is like a tree planted by streams of water. Ps. 1:3, NIV.

The sun was very hot one day as Aaron helped Daddy weed the garden. "Let's rest for a while under the oak tree," Daddy suggested. "It will be cooler there."

Mother brought each of them a glass of water to drink. The water felt good sliding down Aaron's throat. He looked up and saw the huge branches of the tree protecting them from the sun. A squirrel peered down from its nest in the tree.

"Did you know the Bible says that we can be like a tree?" Daddy asked Aaron.

"Yesterday you said our hearts are like a garden," Aaron laughed. "Now we can be like a tree, too?"

"Trees need water just like we do," Daddy said. "Without water we cannot live. Jesus is the water of life. When we ask Jesus into our hearts and when we read the Bible every day, we are growing strong like this tree. Trees provide homes for people and animals. Many trees provide food for us to eat like oranges, pears, apples, and nuts."

"And the tree helps keep us cool," Aaron added. "We can be helpful to others just as this tree is helpful to us."

Daddy patted him on the head. "You're a very smart boy, Aaron. Let's pray that God will help you grow as strong as this tree."

In what ways would you like to be like a tree?—C.B.E.

The Angry Bumblebee

Obey now the voice of the Lord in what I say to you, and it shall be well with you. Jer. 38:20, RSV.

It was such a beautiful day! Not too hot, not too cold. Just plenty of warm sunshine beaming through fluffy, cottony clouds. A shiny green hummingbird darted from one red flower to another. The nectar tasted sweet to the hungry little bird. Jumping up from her chair on the patio, Deanna ran to get a closer look at the tiny bird.

"Mama, do you see the birdie?"

Now, Mama was busy talking to Mrs. Johnson, who lived next door, so she said, "Yes. Isn't it pretty?"

For a little while Deanna happily followed the hummingbird from one bush to another. Then something else caught Deanna's attention.

"Mama, I'm bringing you a surprise." Very carefully Deanna walked over to Mama and Mrs. Johnson. She tenderly held the surprise in her small fingers.

"Buzz . . . buzz . . . buzz . . ." angrily protested the captured insect. "Buzz . . . buzz . . . buzz." The yellow-and-black bumblebee was furious and tried to sting Deanna.

Quickly Mother spoke, "Deanna, let go of the bumblebee right now!" Deanna obeyed instantly. Off flew the bumblebee. Her quick obedience kept Deanna from a stinging pain.

How about you? Will you obey quickly today?—P.M.M.

Jesus' Helpers

Follow me, and I will make you fishers of men. Matt. 4:19.

C hildren," Mommy said, "breakfast is over, and I'm going Ingathering. Would you like to be my partners?"

"Mommy," Elease asked, "what is Ingathering?"

"What?" Kent asked. "Don't you know?"

Before Elease could answer, Byron said, "She's only 3. Elease, we give people a magazine that tells about Bible studies and what our church does for people and ask them to give some money to help buy food and stuff for people who don't have much."

"First we gotta' pray for Jesus to help us, though," Kent chimed in.

"May I pray?" Elease asked.

"Sure," Mother answered.

They all bowed their heads. "Dear Jesus, please help people give money to help somebody else. In Jesus' name, Amen."

"Can we go now, Mom?" Byron asked.

"Yes. Let's get our coats," Mother answered.

Little Elease stayed with Mother, and the boys went across the street. At the first house the people responded to the little girl's special request, "Please help us send money to buy food and stuff for people who don't have as much as we do."

About two hours later, Elease had $8.05, and the two boys had $19.95 between them.

"We're Jesus' helpers," Byron said. "I like being one of Jesus' helpers."

Can you think of a good way to help Jesus?—A.C.B.

A Great Big Ouch

When Jesus had entered Capernaum, a centurion [army commander] came to him. . . . "Lord," he said, "my servant lies at home paralyzed and in terrible suffering." Jesus said to him, "I will go and heal him." Matt. 8:5-7, NIV.

Robby not only liked to build things, but he also liked to take things apart and see if he could put them back together again. So when Dad's big pocket watch stopped working and he had to buy a new one, Dad gave the old one to Robby.

"Oh, boy!" Robby got so excited. "A real watch to work on," he said. He knew that he couldn't fix it, but he could sure have fun.

Robby carefully pried off the back then the glass front. He took off the hands, and one by one took out all the little wheels and gears that had made the old watch run. When he carefully put them in a box to look at later, Robby didn't notice that one of the sharp parts fell to the floor.

"Ouch!" Robby danced around on one foot and grabbed the other bare foot in his hands.

"What's wrong?" Mom asked as she rushed in from the kitchen.

"I stepped on that." He pointed to the little part.

Mom washed the cut and bandaged it. But by nighttime red streaks crept up Robby's ankle and into his leg.

"Oh no! Those are blood poisoning streaks," Mom said. "Dad, we have to get Robby to the doctor right away!"

Robby looked at the red streaks and puffy ankle. He didn't like how it looked. Neither did the doctor, who gave Robby medicine and told him to stay off the foot. That night the family prayed a special prayer for Robby. In a few days his foot was as good as new.

God works with doctors to help us. —C.L.R.

The Honest Mail Carrier

If you abide in My word, you are My disciples indeed. And you shall know the truth, and the truth shall make you free. John 8:31, 32, NKJDV.

Yesterday Mommy paid some postage due on a package. Today the mail carrier rang the doorbell again and handed Carris a dollar. "Please give this to your mother. I made a mistake. She paid me too much, so I'm giving it back."

Carris gave the dollar to Mommy and told her what the letter carrier had said. "That was so good!" Mommy said. "Why, I never would have known the difference."

"Then why didn't he just keep it," Carris wondered aloud, "if nobody knew the difference?"

"*Nobody* knew the difference?" asked Mommy.

"Well, the mail carrier would know the difference." Carris thought for a moment. "And Jesus would know the difference."

Mommy smiled. "Yes indeed. The letter carrier did the right thing by being honest."

Carris did a little dance. "I'm glad we have an honest postal worker. When I grow up, I'm going to be that too."

Mommy was surprised. "You are? I thought you were going to be a fire fighter."

"I am!" laughed Carris. "I meant just the honest part, Mommy, not the mail carrier part."

Mommy gave Carris a huge hug. "And I'll be proud of you no matter what you do. Honest!" she said. —V.L.K.

A Cry for Help

I called on the Lord. . . . The Lord answered me. Ps. 118:5, NKJV.

Twelve-year-old Lennie and his father had been swimming for a while at the beach. The day was pretty, and the water was warm. It was the perfect day for swimming.

Riding the waves was a lot of fun. Lennie and his father would wait for a wave to come in, and then they would let the wave lift them up and take them for a ride. Oh, it was fun and the waves were so strong!

They had been riding the waves when a strong wave hit Lennie's father hard and knocked him down into the water. His father hit his head on a rock and was knocked unconscious.

Lennie, riding the waves, called to his father to watch him. When Lennie didn't see his father he called him again and again. Lennie got scared. He thought, *Is my father drowning? I don't see him. Please, Jesus, help me find my father.*

Frantically, Lennie swam around, looking and calling loudly for his father. "Dad, Dad," he called. But his father didn't answer. Lennie swam around again, and suddenly he spotted the blue color of his father's swim shorts. As he started toward the spot where he saw the blue a wave suddenly washed over him, and that was when he saw his father — lying facedown in the water.

"Dad, Dad," Lennie screamed. "Dear God," he prayed, "help me get my dad out of the water. He's so heavy. Please help me."

Lennie put his arms under his dad's arms, and slowly he began to drag his father out of the water.

Lennie says that God did help him get his dad out of the water that day, saving his life. And Lennie will always thank God for answering his cry for help. —C.B.T.

Angel Unaware

It was a cold winter night. The recent storm left piles and piles of frozen snow on the sides of the road. Nicole and her mother, who was going to have a baby, were driving home from school.

All of a sudden the car hit a sheet of ice and started to slide violently from side to side. The car sped up going down the hill and swerved to the left side of the road, where they could see trees and a deep drop off the side of the road. Sure that they were going over the side, in desperation Nicole's mom cried out, "Jesus, help us!"

Right away they felt the car straighten up and come to a quick stop in the frozen snow right next to the edge of the road.

"Oh, thank You, Jesus, for saving our lives," Nicole and her mother repeated over and over.

God saved Nicole, her mother, and the unborn baby. But they were stuck in the snow, and the car wouldn't move. So they decided to get out and walk home, which was only a short distance away.

Nicole's mother tried to open her door, and Nicole tried to open the other door, but neither would budge. The frozen snow was up to the door. Then they looked out the window.

"Do you see what I see, Nicole?" her mother asked.

"Yes. I see a man walking toward the car," Nicole said. "Look, Mother, it's freezing outside, but he doesn't even have a coat on."

"Oh, but look, he has a shovel in his hand. He's coming closer. He's shoveling the hard, frozen snow from our car!"

When all was clear, the man pointed to go. The car drove beautifully, just as if they had never been stuck.

Nicole looked back to see the man. He was gone! It was a miracle. —E.G.N.

I'm Going to Be a Missionary

Therefore go and make disciples of all nations, baptizing them in the name of the Father and of the Son and of the Holy Spirit, and teaching them to obey everything I have commanded you. And surely I am with you always, to the very end of the age. Matt. 28:19, 20, NIV.

One day Christopher went to Sabbath school. While he was there he sang about a plane that went flying to the mission field.

When Christopher came home from Sabbath school, he said, "Mama, I want to be a missionary. My teacher read from the Bible that we should go and teach all nations. I want to fly on a big plane. I want to go to Singapore, like my cousin Trevor did. I want to take a Bible to the children."

"Oh," said Mama, "not all children can go on a plane to a faraway country. Some children have to stay at home," she said. "But you can still be a missionary. You can be a missionary right at home."

Christopher looked at Mama.

"How can I be a missionary at home, Mama? Missionaries go on planes and boats. They go to countries far away from home."

"Some people go far away to be missionaries," Mama said, "but I know how you can be a missionary right now."

"Tell me, Mama," Christopher said. "How can I be a missionary right now?"

"You can be a missionary by being kind to our neighbors," Mama said.

"What can I do?" Christopher asked.

"Did you see the new people move into the house next door?" Mama said. "You can take them a loaf of the bread that I baked today."

Christopher was happy to take the bread to the new people. He knocked on the door.

A lady came to the door.

"Good morning, little boy," she said.

"Hi!" said Christopher. "I live over there. My name is Christopher. I'm a missionary. I have brought you a loaf of bread. I hope you like it."

"You *are* a real missionary," the lady said, taking the bread from him. "I'm happy for the bread. I have not been able to go to the store yet." She lifted the loaf of bread up to her nose and smelled it. "Oh, it smells so good! My name is Mrs. Murphy. I hope you will visit me again," she said. "I hope you will bring your mama with you."

"Jesus loves you," Christopher said. "And I love you too. I will come again. I will bring my mama with me. Goodbye, Mrs. Murphy."

Christopher was happy. He was a missionary right at home. Christopher did some other things to be a missionary. He shared his *Our Little Friend* with the little girl down the street. He took a friend to Sabbath school with him.

Can you be a missionary just like Christopher?—M.K.S.

Gentle Answer

✷ *A gentle answer quiets anger, but a harsh one stirs it up.* Prov. 15:1, TEV.

"Come on," Teddy cried. "You can't go home now. I like playing basketball."

Dave liked basketball too, but there were other things he had to do. Mother was counting on him to take out the garbage. And his dog, Wheezer, needed to have his walk and then his supper.

"I can't play anymore," Dave explained. "I've got to help my mom."

Teddy made a face. "OK, mama's boy! Go do your little chores!"

Dave could feel his hands wanting to make fists. Sure, he had chores to do, but that didn't make him a mama's boy. Everyone at home did a share of the work. They were a family.

"Go on," Teddy yelled. "I don't need you. I can play better by myself!"

Dave opened his mouth to yell back. He wanted to tell Teddy to shut up and that he was never going to play with him again.

Then Dave remembered something the Sabbath school teacher had explained the other day. She said that it was good to answer angry words with soft ones. That sounded funny to Dave, but usually the teacher was right. Maybe he should try it.

"OK," he told Teddy cheerfully. "If I get done in time, I'll come back and play. OK?"

Teddy looked so surprised that Dave almost laughed. For a minute Teddy didn't say anything. Then he smiled, too. "Sure," he said. "Come back then, and we'll play some more."

Dave went off to do his chores. Next Sabbath he'd have to tell Mrs. Carstairs that the Bible verse was right—soft answers *could* work. —N.C.P.

Let's Be Witnesses!

You are my witnesses. Isa. 43:10, ICB.

D o you know what a witness is? A witness is a person who tells what he or she has seen and heard. Do you know that children like you can be witnesses for Jesus?

Edward is. "Smoking is bad!" Edward almost shouts, pulling himself to his full two feet three inches. Wrinkling his nose, he adds, "Smoking is dirty!" And then, leaning forward, he whispers, "Causes cancer."

Where do you suppose a 4-year-old learned something like that? Edward's mother took him to a stop-smoking program at his church. He saw the doll named Smoking Sam and watched a movie that showed lungs turned black because of cigarette smoking. And he heard a doctor say that cigarette smoking causes lung cancer. Since then Edward has warned his uncle Bill, his uncle Jim, some of his neighbors, and a few strangers whom he saw smoking.

Edward tells people what he has seen and heard so that they can take better care of the bodies God has given to them. What things have you seen or heard that will help someone feel better or be happier? Let's make a list and plan how to share your good news.

1. _____

2. _____

3. _____

—F.J.C.

"He Hit Me!"

✳ *A soft answer turns away wrath, but harsh words cause quarrels.* Prov. 15:1, TLB.

When Timmy started crying, Mommy came running. She gathered her little boy into her arms. She held him close and patted him. "What's the matter?" she asked. But Timmy was crying so hard that he couldn't tell her. So she turned to James. "Why is Timmy crying?"

James shrugged. "He hit me."

Mommy gave James a quick look. "You aren't crying," she said. "I asked why Timmy is crying."

James repeated his statement. "He hit me."

Mommy began to look upset. "If Timmy hit *you*, then why is *he* crying?" she asked.

James looked up at Mommy and smiled. "Well, I had to hit him back, didn't I?"

Mommy sat down in a chair and pulled James close with her other arm. "Have you ever noticed that Timmy is smaller than you? That Timmy is crying? And that you aren't? No, James, you didn't *have* to hit your little brother back."

Do you know that the Bible tells us not to be mean when other people are? When we're mean back, it only makes more trouble. Everyone gets mad, and sometimes we get hurt. If we can be nice when someone else is bad to us, Jesus tells us that the other person will finally be nice to us. You know what else? If we stay nice, then the person who's being bad doesn't have any fun. — V.L.W.

Emily's Shattering Experience

✺ *You are children of God who obey. 1 Peter 1:14, ICB.*

It was almost Daddy's birthday. Mom had placed a package on a high shelf.

I wonder what's inside, Emily thought.

The present was between two of Mommy's favorite things. Mommy had said, "The crystal bowl is very, very old. It was a present that Daddy's mother, Muzzy, was given when she got married."

Next to the bowl was a tall crystal pitcher. "My friend Patricia gave the pitcher to me," she explained. "Now she has died. When I see the pitcher, it reminds me of her."

But the package was beckoning. *Maybe if I could just pick it up, I could guess what is inside*, Emily thought.

As she climbed up on the little brown couch, she thought, *I should be quick so that Mommy doesn't see me.*

Emily felt unsteady on the couch's cushioned surface. *I'll try to steady myself like a tightrope walker does*, she thought.

Crash!

Mother came running, bewildered at the tinkling glass she heard. "Oh, no. Emily, are you all right?"

Emily was halfway under a brown couch cushion with the wooden shelf-top resting over one arm. Slivers of shiny glass were in her hair, dress, and shoes.

Mommy gingerly sifted through the disaster.

"Oh, I didn't mean to do it," Emily sobbed.

Mommy carefully picked away the glass. She didn't find more than a small scratch on Emily's right arm. "Your angel was with you today, Emily," she said in amazement.

"Why haven't you spanked me for breaking your pretty things, Mommy?" Emily asked. "Now you won't be able to remember Muzzy and Patricia anymore."

Mommy looked up in surprise. There were tears in her eyes. "You are more precious to me than all the bowls and pitchers in the world.

I will miss seeing my pretty things, but," she continued, "it would have been far worse if you had been hurt."

At worship that evening Daddy read a story. Jesus searched all night in the storm and cold rain to find a little lost lamb. Jesus didn't scold or punish the lamb.

I'm the naughty little lamb, Emily said to herself. "I want to be a good little lamb. Please help me, Jesus," she prayed. Then Emily lifted her head and smiled. —L.R.

Seeing Inside Someone

My brothers! as believers in our Lord Jesus Christ, the Lord of glory, you must never treat people in different ways according to their outward appearance. James 2:1, TEV.

Gregory was upset. His kindergarten teacher had left to have her baby. The new teacher, Mrs. Albano, had been there for the first time today.

When Gregory got home, he said to Daddy, "I don't like Mrs. Albano at all."

Daddy said, "She's new. You're probably just not used to her yet."

"No," Gregory said. "She's ugly, not pretty like Mrs. Taylor."

Daddy said, "That's no reason to dislike someone. Besides, you haven't even seen what's inside her yet. She may surprise you."

"You need an X-ray to see inside someone, Daddy," Gregory said.

"No, you just need to look with your heart," Daddy replied.

Gregory frowned. Sometimes Daddy said things that were hard to understand. This was one of those times.

Gregory went to school day after day and discovered that he was having a better time than ever. Mrs. Albano was kind and patient. She rarely raised her voice and always seemed to know how to make people feel good, even at sad or lonely moments.

One day Daddy and Gregory were talking about school. "I can't believe I ever said Mrs. Albano was ugly," Gregory said. "My eyes weren't working right, I guess."

Daddy laughed. "You just hadn't looked inside her yet."

Several months went by. A new girl came to school. Amy was pouting.

"What's wrong?" Gregory asked her.

"I miss my old school," Amy answered. "And besides, I don't like the way this teacher looks."

Gregory knew that Amy would change her mind.

"Just wait until you see inside her!" he said. —V.L.K.

"I Will Never Leave You"

☀ *I will never leave you nor forsake you. Heb. 13:5, NKJV.*

A farmer found a wild Canada goose by the riverbank. The bird couldn't fly because his wing had been hurt. The farmer took the goose to the farmyard to get well and named him Voyageur.

Voyageur liked all the animals, chickens, turkeys, and kittens, but he especially liked the tame goose, Priscilla. They made a nest, and he stood guard beside her as she sat on their eggs. Soon after the baby geese hatched, Voyageur's wing healed. Now he could fly again.

About that time a flock of wild Canada geese flew overhead. When Voyageur heard them honking, he flew up and joined them. Priscilla felt so sad because he had left her that she became sick and wouldn't eat for two days. On the third day Voyageur left his wild friends and came back to the farm. Priscilla was so happy to see him that she began to eat and soon got better.

Often Voyageur and Priscilla went to the riverbank to swim. One day the farmer heard the sound of a gun and the scream of a goose. He ran to the river just in time to see a man with a gun get into his car and drive away.

Priscilla lay dead, but Voyageur was not hurt. He sat beside her body. Lovingly he stretched his long neck across her. His eyes looked sad. The farmer dug a grave and laid Priscilla in it. Voyageur watched as the farmer covered Priscilla with dirt. Then Voyageur put his bill into the farmer's hand and cried like a dog.

While they stood beside her grave, they heard the sound of "Honk, Honk!" Voyageur looked up and listened to the wild geese. He had stayed with Priscilla and had not left her side. But now she didn't need him anymore. His strong wings lifted him to join his wild friends.

Jesus is like Voyageur. He will never leave you nor forsake you. You can always trust Jesus to stay with you and take care of you. — E.E.L.

Poor and Naked!

I was naked and you clothed Me; I was sick and you visited Me. . . . And the King will answer, . . . "As you did it to one of the least . . . , you did it to Me." Matt. 25:36-40, NKJV.

Jenny loved to go downtown with Mother. One day while they were shopping for a new dress, Jenny noticed a woman with two children—a little girl and a little boy. All three of them were sitting on a bench. The little girl was crying. She did not have a coat, and her sweater had big holes in it. The little boy tried to comfort her. Jenny noticed that he had bags wrapped around his feet.

"Where are his shoes?" Jenny asked Mother.

"They look very poor," Mother explained. "Maybe he doesn't have any shoes."

Jenny's eyes opened wide. "No shoes!" she said.

"Some children are so poor that they don't have a nice home to live in or a bed to sleep in. These people look homeless."

Jenny thought about her warm bed at home. She thought about her closet full of pretty clothes. "Mother," she said, "please don't buy me a new dress. Let's go buy that little boy a pair of shoes instead."

In what ways can you clothe and feed Jesus?—C.B.E.

Faithful Fidel

☼ *Be faithful until death, and I will give you the crown of life. Rev. 2:10, NKJV.*

Fidel was a skinny black-and-white dog with a cute bushy tail that curled over. One day Fidel's owner went away on a boat and left him all alone on the beach. Poor Fidel! He put his tail between his legs and cried like a baby.

"Don't cry. Come home with us," said Catherine and Florence as they patted the little dog. They were missionaries who lived in a little room in a tiny church. "We don't have much to give you—except love."

But that was enough. Fidel was happy in his new home. He loved his new owners so much that he would cry whenever they left the room. "Let's call him Fidel," said Catherine, "because he is so faithful."

One day Catherine and Florence decided that it was time for them to return to their home country. "What are we going to do?" they wondered. "Dear Jesus," they prayed, "please help this dog love somebody else so that when we go he won't be standing on the beach crying."

When they met Veronica, a little girl who had lots of pets, they thought, *Maybe she is the answer to our prayers.* Catherine asked her, "Would you like to have this nice dog?"

"Oh, yes," Veronica said.

"We'll be leaving on the boat tomorrow at 5:00 p.m. You'll hear the whistle," Catherine told her. "Then you can let Fidel out. But don't let him out before then, because he will find us."

The next morning Catherine and Florence slipped out quietly to pass out tracts. But before long, they heard, "Ruff, ruff." Can you guess what it was? It was Fidel. Fidel was faithful. He couldn't bear to be apart from Catherine and Florence. He loved them dearly.

That's how we ought to feel about Jesus. Do you?—P.H.

Fidel Finds a Home

※ Ask and it will be given to you. Matt. 7:7, NIV.

Remember Fidel? And how he kept finding his way back to his owners? Are you wondering whatever happened to him? Here's the rest of the story.

Catherine and Florence carried Fidel right back to Veronica. Catherine reminded her to keep Fidel inside until 5:00 that evening. Then the dog would be hers to keep.

About 3:00 p.m. the two missionary ladies went to get some supper at a little restaurant. Soon they heard the familiar bark again. It was Fidel! So they gave him a little tortilla and delivered him for the second time to Veronica.

By 5:00 that evening, Catherine and Florence were ready to get on the boat and leave. Florence turned to Catherine and said, "If he comes again, we'll take him with us."

Just then they looked down the road and saw a little black streak racing toward them. What could it be? Yes, it was Fidel! So Catherine said, "God must have a different way of answering our prayers, because it looks like Fidel will be going with us." And so he did.

But back on their home island it wasn't long before they discovered how God would answer their prayer. One day as Catherine and Florence were walking down the street, Fidel let out a happy squeal. Fidel recognized the man to whom he used to belong. "Would you like to have Fidel back?" they asked. And, of course, the man said he would.

Two happy missionaries knew that Fidel had a loving, safe place to live, and they were thankful that God does answer prayers. —P.H.

Mrs. Wheeler and Mrs. Grant

My heart took delight in all my work. Eccl. 2:10, NIV.

Rrrrrring. Rrrrrrring." Connie held her pretend telephone up to her ear. She lived way out in the country and didn't have a real telephone at her house. "Rrrrrrring. Mrs. Wheeler? This is Mrs. Grant."

Mother answered from the kitchen. "Oh, hello, Mrs. Grant. How are you today?"

"I'm fine. What are you doing?" Connie asked from the living room.

"I'm getting ready to bake cookies. Would you like to come over and visit me and help me?"

"Yes!" Connie hung up her pretend telephone and ran to the kitchen. Soon she and Mom had flour on their hands, and Connie even had a dab on her nose. Even though she was only 5 years old, she knew just how to cut out sugar cookies, because Mother had let her help ever since she was big enough to hold the cutter. During all the time they worked, they talked.

"Mrs. Wheeler, you work hard, don't you?"

"Oh yes, Mrs. Grant. But I like to work. I like seeing lines of my family's clean clothes whipping in the wind. I like the smell of polished furniture and clean floors."

"And *I* like the smell of warm cookies!" Connie sniffed. "You sing while you work. Are you happy?"

"Very." Mother hugged her little girl. "You are such a big help! And Dad and the boys always appreciate what I do. I'm glad God picked me to be in this family and no other."

"Me, too, Mother." Connie hugged Mother back and reached for a cookie. —C.L.R.

Marty's Marvelous Maple Seed

For where light is, there all goodness springs up, all justice and truth. Eph. 5:9, NEB.

A seed from a maple tree stuck to Marty's shoe, and he acciden-tally planted it on the dirt floor of the shed. One day Marty noticed a tiny tree growing there. He watered it every day, but the tree began to wither and shrink.

Marty ran to his father. "My little tree is dead!" he cried.

"Let's have a look," Daddy said.

They hurried to the shed. Daddy knelt down near the tree. "It's not quite dead," he said, "but it will be if we leave it here."

Very carefully Daddy dug up the tiny tree. Then he transplanted it to the sunniest spot in the backyard. "There. Now it's in the light, so it should live and grow."

"Daddy," said Marty, "I didn't know trees were like people."

"Like people?" Daddy questioned.

"Yes," Marty answered. "I remember from Bible class that Jesus is called the Light of the world. If you don't have His light in you, you can't live and grow."

Daddy smiled his warmest, proudest smile. "Marty," he said, "I know you'll live and grow wonderfully, just like your marvelous maple seed."

Marty's hair gleamed in the sunshine. And inside he glowed from a different kind of light. —V.L.K.

Buttons

He will wipe every tear from their eyes. Rev. 21:4, NIV.

Here, Buttons, I have some dandelion leaves for you," Priska said as she ran to the cage of her fluffy white lop-eared bunny. His button nose twitched as he munched on his treat. That's how he got his name. When Priska would go to his cage, he would come to her and let her rub his button nose. "I love you, Buttons! You are so soft and warm. I'm glad Jesus gave you to me," Priska whispered to Buttons.

Buttons stayed outside in a sturdy cage called a hutch, and every day Priska would give him a treat of something green like clovers, dandelions, or lettuce, and she would check to see if he had enough water to drink and rabbit pellets to eat.

Years passed, and Priska's mommy noticed that Buttons didn't move as fast as he used to, and when he was held, lots of fur would come off him. Buttons was getting old. Priska's mother would sometimes talk to her about what happens when animals get old, and Priska knew that Buttons would die someday. It would make her sad to think about it, and a tear would drop down her cheek.

One morning Priska went out to Buttons' cage to check on him. When she came to the cage, she didn't see his whiskers twitching. His button nose didn't move. He didn't even hop over to let her pat him. Priska reached her hand into the cage, and Buttons' fur wasn't warm and soft anymore. He was cold and hard. Buttons was dead.

Priska's legs couldn't carry her fast enough back into the house to tell her mother about Buttons. Tears ran down her face, and she sobbed as she told all about her Buttons.

But we have the hope of having lots of pets in heaven. You may have lost a pet, and felt sad, and cried. That's OK. It is all right to cry. One day we will be in heaven, where there will be no more crying or dying. —E.G.N.

Feed the Hungry

I was hungry and you fed me. Matt. 25:35, TEV.

Donnie watched Mom putting groceries in the bag. "What are those for?" he asked.

"I'm taking them to Sabbath services," Mother said.

"Why? Are we having a dinner today?"

"No," Mother said. "We're taking them because sometimes people who are hungry come to us for food."

"Why can't they get food for themselves?" Donnie asked.

"We don't know. We just know that they're hungry. And we know that we should feed them," Mother explained.

Donnie didn't understand that. "But Mother, if we don't know these people, why should we feed them?"

Mother put a jar of jelly in the big brown bag of groceries. "We feed them because Jesus said we should. Jesus cares about everyone, you know, especially about people who don't have much."

The grocery bag was full clear to the very top. Mother reached for her coat. "Bring that big jar of peanut butter, too."

Donnie put on his coat and picked up the jar. He was glad Mother had put jelly in the bag. Peanut butter and jelly made his favorite sandwiches.

"Actually," Mother said, turning to lock the door behind them, "Jesus said when we feed the hungry, it's like we're feeding Him."

Donnie looked down at the peanut butter and smiled. Jesus would like peanut butter and jelly too. —N.C.P.

No More Goodbyes

❉ *The Lord God will wipe away every tear from every face. Isa.*
25:8, ICB.

No books, no toys—just clothes," Herb whispered the instructions again. "I hate leaving my treasure," Herb said to himself.
"But so do Mom and Dad and my two brothers. And we all hate
leaving Lassie. But there's a war going on!"

"Arf! Arf!" the collie called the family to play. It was springtime
in Shanghai, China.

Sniff! Sniff! Then Herb coughed. It was hard work for a 9-year-old
boy to keep from crying. He turned to wipe a tear off his nose before
anyone could see it. Then he saw Mother wiping her eyes. "Let's take
a break, Herb," Mother said. "We've got to say goodbye to a friend!"

"Mom says let's play with Lassie!" Herb called to his brothers.

"Yea!" they shouted and raced past him.

Dad joined them. The cook, Gou Cin Chou, and his family came
out to watch the fun too. After a round of running and jumping with
Lassie, Herb noticed Mother hugging Mrs. Chou. All at once everyone was hugging someone. Dad promised to pray for the Chous. And
the Chous said they would never forget the missionaries.

Before long the Larsens were seated in a barge being towed down
the Yellow River. Then they boarded a ship named the *U.S. President
Washington* and sailed for the Philippine Islands, along with 3,000
Marines.

"This gum is great!" Herb told a friendly Marine. "We never had
gum in China!"

The boys enjoyed talking and laughing with the Marines. But too
soon it was time to tell them goodbye in the Philippines and continue
their trip to America.

"Goodbye! Goodbye! Goodbye! I hate saying goodbye," Herb
mumbled. But he waved to the Marines until they were out of sight.

Even after he finally arrived in the United States, Herb and his
family moved several times. He grew up and became a Seventh-day

Adventist minister. So he still has to say goodbye many times as he goes from place to place so that he can tell others about Jesus. Sometimes a tear slips down his nose.

"But one day very soon Jesus will come," says Elder Herb Larsen. "Then we'll never again have to say goodbye to our friends and loved ones. Won't that be wonderful?"

[Note to parents: Herbert S. Larsen is secretary of the Lake Union Conference.]—F.J.C.

Broken Things

☀ *For your heart will always be where your riches are. Luke 12:34, TEV.*

"I hate Jay," said Seth.

"Hate him?" Mommy asked. "Jay is your best friend."

"No, he's not. He broke my truck."

"It was an accident, Seth," said Mommy. "He didn't mean it. He said he was sorry."

"I don't care," said Seth, pouting. "Now I need a new truck *and* a new best friend."

The next day Jay didn't come over. Playing alone wasn't as much fun as playing together, and Seth felt lonely. But he was still upset with Jay.

After lunch Mommy said, "Aunt Grace made some strawberry shortcake, and she wants us to come over and have some."

"Yippee!" said Seth.

After they had eaten, Seth played with the circus train in the living room while Mommy and Aunt Grace talked in the kitchen.

Seth pretended that the circus monkey escaped—over the couch, around the coffee table, up onto the end table, and *crash!*

Aunt Grace's beautiful, expensive lamp shattered against the fireplace.

"The monkey . . . I was just trying to chase him. . . . I didn't mean it," Seth sobbed.

Aunt Grace hugged Seth. "Of course you didn't, honey. We all have accidents. I'm just glad you didn't get hurt."

Seth couldn't believe it. He had broken Aunt Grace's favorite lamp, and she still loved him!

"The lamp was so valuable," Mommy groaned.

"Nonsense!" said Aunt Grace. "Nothing I own is more valuable than friendship."

On the way home Seth thought about valuable things and broken things.

"I'm going to Jay's," he said.

"Good idea!" Mommy said with a smile. —V.L.K.

Run Over by a Car

For he orders his angels to protect you wherever you go. They will steady you . . . to keep you from stumbling against the rocks on the trail. Ps. 91:11, 12, TLB.

"Stop! Stop! You ran over my brother!" I screamed.

I cried all the way to the house, "Don't let my brother die, dear Jesus. Please don't let him die!"

It all started when Uncle Wilson and Daddy took us for a ride. Just before we got home, the old V-8 gave a cough and a wheeze and died.

"Looks like it could use some gasoline," said Daddy.

"Well," said Uncle Wilson, "guess we'll have to push it to the station. You big kids hop out and walk to the house so that the car won't be so heavy."

He and Daddy started pushing the car. Kids began spilling out the doors and windows—I guess we all thought we were the "big kids." But 3-year-old Melvin fell out onto the pavement right in front of the car's back wheel.

"Oh no!" I screamed as I saw the back tire run right over his little legs! I was sure he would die. Mother had always warned us, "If you get hit by a car, you'll die."

When I screamed, Uncle Wilson stopped the car, and Daddy ran to scoop Melvin up in his arms. My brother's little legs just dangled as Daddy rushed him to the house, and he kept saying, "Don't let me die!" He lay still for quite a while, but soon he was running around like nothing ever happened to him. No blood, no broken bones. *He was not going to die!* And I stopped crying.

I never asked for a baby brother. In fact, I didn't really want one. And sometimes he could be such a pest! But after this happened, when he teased me or broke my dolls or messed up my playhouse, I always tried to remember how I felt the day I thought he was going to die.

And I often thank Jesus for sending the angels to protect him that day the car ran over him. —B.V.

God Doesn't Sleep

✳ *He who watches over you will not slumber. Ps. 121:3, NIV.*

Please don't turn off the light," Timmy begged one night when Mother tucked him into bed. "I don't like the dark."

"But why, Timmy?" Mother asked. "The dark is very friendly. You'll sleep better in the dark."

"But I'm afraid," Timmy said, and he began to cry.

Mother sat beside Timmy on the bed and held him close. "There's no need for you to be afraid. Your daddy and I are right down the hall. We will watch over you and keep you safe."

"But you and Daddy can't watch me while you are sleeping," Timmy said.

Mother smiled. "You're right. But do you remember the story I told you about Daniel and how the king lowered Daniel into the lions' den?"

Timmy nodded. "He did it because Daniel prayed to God instead of the king. It must have been dark down there under the ground."

"That's right, Timmy. And it must have been scary to sleep with a bunch of hungry lions. God sent His angel to shut the lions' mouths and to keep Daniel safe. The Bible says that God doesn't sleep. He is always watching over you and me."

What should you do when you are afraid?—C.B.E.

Getting New Clothes

There is a time for everything. Eccl. 3:1, NIV.

"It's time to think about getting new school clothes for you children," Dad told Tina and Jeff.

"Good." But Jeff's mouth turned down a little. "Uh, Dad, is there enough money?"

"If we're careful." Dad sighed. Raising two children on a small salary wasn't easy. "Let's watch for special sales."

"We aren't the only ones getting new clothes," Jeff said and grinned. "Tina, look at that." He pointed to a big maple tree out the window that had already started to drop yellow leaves. "The tree's green leaf coat is yellow now."

Tina eagerly joined the game. "And our dog's coat will get thicker pretty soon when the weather starts getting cold."

"Snakes shed their skins and grow new ones," Jeff said.

"Ugh! You can have your old snakes." Tina made a face.

"Squirrels get heavier coats too. And I read in a book at school that some rabbits up north turn white in winter so they can't be seen against the snow."

"Dad, how come fur gets thicker only when winter is coming?" Tina wanted to know. "Is there an alarm clock inside our dog Toby and the squirrels and bears and other animals that says when it's time for their fur to grow thick?"

Jeff laughed and laughed, but Dad just said, "Not exactly. However, God created animals so they'd be protected."

"I'm glad," Jeff said, and patted Toby's head. —C.L.R.

Dolls and Bicycles

✶ *Forgive, and you will be forgiven. Luke 6:37, NKJV.*

Sarajane was sitting alone on the porch of her house. Her best friend, Sally, had just told her, "I don't want to play with you anymore, Sarajane. You're mean."

The two friends had argued over what game to play. Sarajane had wanted to play dolls, but Sally had wanted them to ride their bicycles. They had argued, and now the two friends were mad at each other. Sally had gone home to her house, which was next door to Sarajane's house, and now Sarajane was all by herself, with no one to play with.

Sarajane was sad. Sarajane was lonely. She had no one to play with. But most of all Sarajane was lonely for her friend. As Sarajane sat on the porch of her house, she was remembering what Mommy had said about being kind to others. Jesus was kind to everyone, even to the people who didn't obey Him.

Mommy had said that Jesus is happy when we try to be like Him. Sarajane wanted to be like Jesus, but sometimes it was hard. Sarajane loved Jesus, and she had asked Jesus to help her be good and kind when her family had prayed that morning. But now she and Sally were mad at each other, and that sure was not being like Jesus.

Sitting on her front porch, Sarajane prayed, "Dear Jesus, I want to be like You. I'm so sorry that I hurt my friend. I miss her. Help me be kind to her. Thank You. Amen."

Sarajane got up from the porch and walked over to her friend's yard. She walked slowly up the steps and knocked on the front door. Sally's mother came to the door. "Why, hello, Sarajane. How are you?"

"Hello, Mrs. Walker. I'm all right. I came to see Sally. We had a fight, and I have come to ask her to forgive me and to please come and play with me again."

"Why, Sarajane, that's very nice of you! Come in. I'll call Sally."

Mrs. Walker went into Sally's bedroom to call her. Soon Sally came to the door. She walked with her head down and slowly came to the living room, where Sarajane was standing.

"Hello, Sally," said Sarajane. "Uh . . . I'm sorry that I yelled at you. Uh . . . please forgive me. I want us to be friends again."

Sally, with her head still bowed, said, "I'm sorry I yelled at you, Sarajane. Please forgive me too."

They looked at each other and smiled. Then Sally said, "I missed you. I was so lonely with no one to play with. You're my best friend, Sarajane."

"Let's go and play. We can play dolls *and* ride our bikes," said Sarajane happily.

Together the girls went outside to play. They were happy that they were friends again. And happy that Jesus was helping them be like Him. —C.B.T.

Love Won

There is no fear in love, but perfect love casts out fear.
1 John 4:18, RSV.

Two big boys, hiking in the mountains, saw a baby eagle in its nest. When the mother eagle flew far away, they climbed up to the nest, threw a sack over the little eagle, and although it was against the law, they took it home for a pet. They named him Butch.

But Butch didn't like his cage. He wanted his mother. He wanted to live in the woods. He felt afraid of people and wouldn't drink water or eat the food the boys gave him. When they came near, he tried to bite them with his strong beak or scratch them with his sharp toes.

"I'm sorry we took Butch from his mother," said the older boy. "I'm afraid he'll die because he won't eat. We can't take him back to his nest. Maybe the kindest thing would be to kill him, or he will slowly starve to death."

When they returned with a gun, little brother Jimmy stood by the cage. "Please don't kill Butch. I love him. Jesus will show me how to take away Butch's fear so that he'll want to drink and eat," Jimmy said.

Jimmy prayed to Jesus for help. Then walking closer to the cage, he talked softly to Butch. The little eagle didn't move. Slowly Jimmy reached his hand into the cage and touched the feathers on Butch's head. Instead of biting Jimmy, the bird seemed to enjoy the touch of love. Jimmy kept talking and patting the baby bird gently. The bird liked the love. With his other hand Jimmy held some food next to the sharp beak. Butch took it, and later he drank water.

Never again did the eagle try to hurt anyone. He became part of the family, even sleeping with the dog. Love took away the bird's fear.

Jesus wants to take away your fear too. If you're afraid of the dark, afraid of being alone, or afraid of *anything*, tell Jesus about it. He loves you. He will come near you like Jimmy did Butch. His love will take away your fears. —E.E.L.

Foster Mothers

I will not leave you as orphans; I will come to you. John 14:18, NIV.

Tamika's new foster mother was tucking her into bed. "How long will you take care of me?" Tamika asked.

Mrs. Jackson touched Tamika's cheek gently. "For as long as you need me," she answered.

"Good," Tamika said. Before Tamika fell asleep she said an extra prayer, asking Jesus to give her foster mother a special blessing.

The next morning Tamika and Mrs. Jackson took a walk in the field. They picked a bouquet of wildflowers. There were black-eyed Susans and golden buttercups, snow-white baby's breath and sky-blue forget-me-nots.

Mrs. Jackson said, "Come here. There's something I want you to see." They crossed the road to the Salisbury farm.

"Look at that mother duck with her babies," Mrs. Jackson said.

Tamika noticed right away. "Why is that one duck so much bigger than the other four?"

Mrs. Salisbury had told Mrs. Jackson about the unusual family, so she explained to Tamika. "That baby duck is really a goose, that's why. After a fox attacked a goose's nest, there was only one egg left. So Mrs. Salisbury put it under the mother duck, and it hatched. Now the mother duck takes care of it just as if it were her very own."

Tamika smiled brightly and said, "God takes care of everyone and everything, doesn't He?"

Mrs. Jackson gripped Tamika's hand and smiled too. "Yes, He certainly does," she agreed.

Tamika laughed out loud. "That baby goose sure is blessed. It has a wonderful foster mother—just like me!"—V.L.K.

I Am Wonderfully Made

⚹ *I will give thanks to Thee, for I am fearfully and wonderfully made.* Ps. 139:14, NASB.

Have you ever been to a lake or to the ocean and watched the birds? If you are very quiet and don't move too much or too quickly, you can see the birds looking for food.

Some ducks put their heads down until their bills touch the top of the water so that they can eat the seeds and small insects that float on the water. Other ducks, when they look for food, put their heads all the way into the water. When they see a nice fish swim by, they dive under the water to get it.

The beautiful pink flamingos use their long necks to hold their heads upside down in the water. This is the way they catch tiny animals to eat. Snowy egrets splash around in the mud with their long legs as they look for animals that might be hiding.

Many different kinds of water birds can live together because they don't eat the same foods. God made them different. He made them special.

We are each different too. We like to eat different things. Some people like oranges best of all. Others like apples. What fruit do you like best?

God has made each of us special, and He loves us for our special ways. See if you can find pictures of the different things that you like. —M.M.M.

Stuck in the Mud

For with God nothing will be impossible. Luke 1:37, NKJV.

It was a crisp, damp morning in Maryland. The night's rainfall had blown red, yellow, and orange leaves everywhere. We could tell that the ground was soggy and wet by looking at the raindrops glittering on the grass and leaves.

Nevertheless, six day-care children and three of my own piled into the car to see what was still growing in our garden plot in the nearby woods. The unpaved road in the garden area was muddy, but the car rolled over the mud, giving us a smooth ride. The children jumped up and down in excitement, yelling, "I see something green!"

I opened the car door, and we all explored what was left of the garden. It didn't take us long to gather some greens, a few green tomatoes, and some peppers.

We got into the car again and started for home. The car moved slowly, and the sound of spinning wheels and mud splattering everywhere filled our ears. We gradually came to a stop and just rocked in the mud.

Although the children's eyes bulged, their tight lips revealed only silence. Then I announced, "I think we are stuck." I got out to examine just how stuck we were. Believe me, we were stuck! The once tan car with four wheels now appeared to be a brown polka dotted car with no wheels. I got back into the car and said, "Yes, we are stuck!"

"Jesus can get us out," the children chimed in unison.

"Surely, Jesus can get us out," I agreed.

We prayed. Waited a few minutes. No one came to help us. I started the car and pressed on the gas pedal. The car rocked back and forth, then suddenly lunged backward, as if being pushed by someone. We were out of the mud!

As we joyfully drove home, we sang, "Thank You, Jesus, for getting us out of the mud."—E.G.N.

Love

Your life must be controlled by love, just as Christ loved us. Eph. 5:2, TEV.

Andy stared after Joe. Sometimes his big brother made him mad. Why did Joe have to be nasty? Andy was big enough to go to the park too, if only Joe would take him along.

But Joe always said no, and Andy had to stay home. It just wasn't fair. He slammed the front door and stomped up to his room. *Joe is just mean, nasty!* thought Andy as he slammed the door to his room and threw himself onto his bed. He'd fix Joe! He'd find a way to get even.

A few minutes later Mother knocked on the door. "Andy?"

Andy sat up. "Yes, Mother."

Mother opened the door and came in. "What's wrong, Andy?"

"It's Joe. He wouldn't take me to the park. He's so mean."

Mother sat down beside him. "He doesn't want to look out for you."

"I'm big," Andy said. "I can take care of myself."

Mother nodded. "I know. In a year or two you can go to the park by yourself."

A year was a long, long time. Too long. Andy made his hands into fists. "I hate Joe!" he cried. "I'm going to fix him!"

Mother frowned. "Andy, you mustn't hate. And getting even is not a good thing."

"Joe's mean to *me*. Why can't *I* be mean to him?"

"Because," Mother said, "the Bible tells us that our lives must be controlled by love. Jesus loves us. And He wants us to love other people."

Andy thought about that. How could he love Joe when Joe was so mean to him? "But Mother, it's hard."

Mother smiled. "I know. Just think how hard it was for Jesus. People were really mean to Him. But He forgave them."

Andy thought some more. Then he uncurled his fists. "I guess I'll have to get over being mad at Joe. Jesus wouldn't be mad."

"You're right," Mother said, giving him a hug. "You're so right."—N.C.P.

The Ugly Tomato Worm

I am making everything new! Rev. 21:5, NIV.

When my granddaughter Julie was small, I found a big, fat, ugly, green tomato worm.

"I don't like it," she said. "It's yucky."

"Let's take care of it," I said. "Maybe Jesus will make it pretty."

Suddenly she got interested in the fat, green worm. "Her name's Dotty," Julie said. "Let's make her a nice home." We put the worm in a gallon jar containing two inches of dirt and some tomato vines.

We gave Dotty fresh tomato leaves every day. But one day she was gone. We lifted the jar and found her—all curled up under the dirt.

"Dotty's sleeping," I told Julie. "When she wakes up, I bet Jesus will have made her pretty."

Julie could hardly wait for Jesus to make the ugly worm pretty. One day we found a big furry gray-and-pink moth sitting in the jar.

I lifted the moth onto Julie's finger, where she could watch it. "Where did it come from?" she asked.

I hugged her close. "Jesus turned Dotty into this beautiful moth," I said. "Really, He did. He's coming back to this earth, sweetie. And He'll make everything beautiful. And no one will be sick or crippled anymore."

We took the big moth outside. Julie held her hand high so that the moth could fly free.

"Hurry and come back, Jesus," she said after the moth disappeared from sight. —V.L.W.

Skunks Are Not Bad

Do not judge others, so that God will not judge you. Matt. 7:1, TEV.

Many people say bad things about a beautiful black-and-white animal called a skunk. True, skunks do try to protect themselves by sending out a very bad smell when someone wants to hurt them. But if you do not move fast or scare them, they will be nice to you.

The Hoyt family lived in a cabin in the woods. One evening when they were eating supper, a skunk walked in through the open door. What should they do? They didn't want a bad smell in their house. Mrs. Hoyt put some milk in a bowl, set it on the table, and pulled up a chair. Right away the skunk jumped up onto the chair and began drinking the milk.

Almost every night the skunk came for a bowl of milk. If the door was shut, he thumped on it with his feet or made noises to be let in. They named him Little Corporal. Then one day he didn't come. They missed him.

Several weeks later they heard a thump on the door again. When they opened it, they found Little Corporal, Mrs. Corporal, and six baby skunks. Mrs. Corporal seemed afraid and began thumping the floor. The babies followed. Would they send out the bad smell? Little Corporal looked around and jumped up on the chair. He pounded the table with his front feet. Mrs. Hoyt gave him a bowl of milk right away. Then she put bowls of milk on the floor for the mama and the babies.

Many times after that the skunk family came to visit and get their milk. Not once did they ever leave a bad smell.

Remember the skunk family when you hear someone say something bad about others. Don't believe it. Instead, say something good. Jesus says, "Don't judge others. Say only kind things."—E.E.L.

Tim Helps the Flowers Grow

☀ *Whatever your hand finds to do, do it with all your might. Eccl. 9:10, NIV.*

They're beautiful," Tim whispered to Grandpa Halvorsen as they entered the Pioneer Memorial church. For a moment they stood there admiring the pink and yellow and red and white gladiolus. Tim could tell that the other people nearby liked his flowers too. The look on their faces said, "Those flowers are beautiful!" Even an 8-year-old boy like Tim knew that look.

Well they should be beautiful! Tim thought. *Grandpa and I worked hard to grow them.*

This is what Tim and Grandpa Halvorsen did.

In the spring Tim planted the flower bulbs three inches apart. "Be sure the points of the bulbs are turned upward," Tim reminded himself as he crawled along in the dirt. The hot sun turned his light-brown hair blond. And the brown dirt stuck under his fingernails.

In the days that followed, Tim helped dig up all the weeds that would choke the flowers. And he prayed, "Dear Jesus, please send the sunshine and rain so that our flowers will grow."

When the gladiolus began to bloom, Tim started work each morning at 6:00. "That's even earlier than some fathers and mothers go to work," Tim sometimes told himself. "But I have to start early. It takes a long time to cut the flowers, carry them to the garage, and sort them into bundles."

During the week, Tim and Grandpa sold flowers to fruit stands along Highway 31-33 from Niles to St. Joseph, Michigan. On most Sabbaths, like today, they took a vase of flowers to church.

Tim and Grandpa found a seat near the piano. Then Tim heard a woman in the next pew say, "What beautiful flowers!"

Tim smiled. Grandpa leaned over and whispered in Tim's ear, "Thanks again for your good work, Tim."

How do you know when people think you have done a good job? [Their words, hugs, smiles.] How do you let people know when you think they have done a good job?

[Note to parents: Timothy Roosenberg is pastor of the Hagerstown, Maryland, Seventh-day Adventist Church.]—F.J.C.

The Broken Lamp

☀ *The law of truth was in his mouth. Mal. 2:6, NKJV.*

Nicholas had been playing with his ball in the dining room at Grandfather's house. He bounced the ball higher and higher until the ball hit the lamp hanging from the ceiling. The lamp broke. Nicholas felt scared—and sorry.

Nicholas knew he must tell Pop-Pop, his grandfather, about the broken lamp. And he knew that Pop-Pop would want to know how the lamp got broken.

Nicholas had been taught that no matter what you did, whether it was good or bad, you should tell the truth. With a heavy sigh Nicholas went to tell his grandfather about the broken lamp.

Pop-Pop was sitting in the living room, reading a book, when Nicholas came in.

"Um, Pop-Pop," said Nicholas softly. Pop-Pop didn't hear Nicholas. "Pop-Pop," Nicholas said a little louder. This time Pop-Pop heard Nicholas, and he looked up from his book.

"Yes, Nicholas?"

"Um, Pop-Pop, I was playing ball in the dining room, and I bounced the ball too hard, and it . . . broke the lamp in the dining room."

Pop-Pop looked at his grandson and said, "Nicholas, I'm sorry you were playing ball in the house, especially when you were told not to do that. And I'm sorry you broke the lamp, but I'm glad that you have come to me and told me about it."

Pop-Pop looked at Nicholas for a little while. "Now, Nicholas, what do you think we ought to do about the broken lamp?" Pop-Pop asked.

Nicholas said, "Pop-Pop, I will pay for the lamp out of the money I saved in my piggy bank."

Pop-Pop looked at his grandson and said, "Nicholas, because you came and told me the truth and because you're willing to pay for the lamp with your own money, I'll tell you what I'll do. *I* will pay for the lamp. You're a good boy because you were so honest with me."

Nicholas was a happy little boy.

A few years have passed since Nicholas broke the lamp, but he still remembers how his grandfather told him that he was proud of him because he came and told him the truth even when he had done something wrong.

Sometimes you may not always want to tell the truth after you have done something bad, and you may be afraid, but Jesus wants boys and girls to be honest and always to tell the truth. —C.B.T.

Moving Day

Happiness makes a person smile. Prov. 15:13, ICB.

Daddy brought Mother and the twins, Cody and Cory, from the airport. "This is your new home," he said. The house was a lot bigger than their apartment had been.

"And this is your room," said Mother.

Cody and Cory peeked inside. All their toys were there and their beds.

"It doesn't feel like home," said Cody.

"We don't want to live here," said Cory.

"You'll get used to it soon," said Daddy. "Go outside and see the big backyard you have to play in."

Cory and Cody felt sad as they walked down the hall and out the back door. Then Cory saw the tire swing in the big apple tree. And Cody found a pile of dirt just right for filling dump trucks and building roads. They looked behind the drooping weeping willow tree branches that hung to the ground.

"This will make a good camp," said Cody.

Suddenly they heard a noise. They ran to see what it was. They found a box by the back steps that wasn't there before. The noise was coming from inside. Before the boys could reach it, the box toppled over, and out popped a ball of brown fur.

"A puppy!" the boys shouted at the same time. The puppy barked and ran.

Laughing and shouting, Cody and Cory chased the puppy around the yard until they were all tired out. Still laughing, the boys fell in a heap. The puppy jumped on them. He licked their faces with a quick, pink tongue. Then he barked and bounced around them, begging to be chased.

"I think he likes it here," said Cody.

"I like this new home," said Cory, grinning.

Cody grinned back. "Me too," he agreed. —M.H.D.

The Globe Game

☀ *God lives in us and his love is perfected in us.* 1 John 4:17, NRSV.

Noah and Mama were spinning a globe of the world.

Noah pointed to Australia. "Kangaroos and koalas live in Australia. Don't you wish you lived there?" Noah asked Mama.

"No," she answered.

Noah pointed to South America. "There are fuzzy llamas and beautiful toucans in South America. Don't you wish you lived there?" Noah asked.

"No," Mama answered.

Noah pointed to the top of North America. "Polar bears and timber wolves live near the North Pole. Don't you wish you lived there?" he asked.

"No," Mama answered.

Noah pointed to Africa. "Hippos and elephants live in Africa," he said. Then he pointed to Asia. "And giant pandas that eat bamboo live in Asia. Don't you wish you lived there, either?" Noah asked.

"No," Mama answered again with a smile. "I'm happiest right here in our own little town."

"Why?" Noah asked.

Mama touched Noah on the nose. "Because the best little boy in the whole wide world lives here," she said.

And Noah and Mama ended their globe game with a huge, round hug. —V.L.K.

I'm Not Too Small

☼ Be kind to one another. Eph. 4:32, RSV.

Did you know that you don't have to be big to be a helper? Even though the tickbird is only about the size of a spoon, it helps big animals like rhinoceroses, buffaloes, and giraffes. Tickbirds help keep these animals clean.

Tickbirds like to stay on the backs of big animals. They dig around on the animals' backs, looking for insects. As they find insects, they eat them. This helps the rhinoceroses, buffaloes, and giraffes get rid of some of the insects that bother them.

When the animals that the tickbirds ride on are in danger, tickbirds fly around, crying loudly and telling the animal that danger is near. A tickbird's bill is sharp like a pair of scissors. If the animal gets hurt, the tickbird helps the animal by using its sharp bill to fix the wound.

Even though you are small, you can be a helper too. You can help Mommy and Daddy by picking up your toys, by playing nicely, and even by making Mommy and Daddy laugh. God wants you to be His helper too. He wants you to be kind to everybody.

Ask your mommy and daddy if you may help them today. — M.M.M.

How Embarrassing!

They looked to Him and were radiant, and their faces were not ashamed. Ps. 34:5, NKJV.

Patty's fluffy blonde curls bounced as she skipped along the sidewalk leading up to the church. Patty knew that she must keep her dress clean and not step in the mud. No, she shouldn't jump over the puddle, either. When you go into Jesus' house, you should look your best.

But why was Mama taking so long? wondered Patty. She just went to get her purse in the car. The parking lot wasn't that far away. Patty was feeling alone.

Patty looked up. Daddy was standing in front of the church while he was talking to some men. He had on his dark-blue suit, and his shirt had tiny stripes going up and down. Whew! She would run over and stand next to Daddy. Then she wouldn't feel all alone.

Coming close to Daddy, Patty reached up and took Daddy's big hand in hers.

"Well, aren't you a sweet little girl," boomed a big voice. Looking up, Patty saw that the hand she was holding was *not* her dad's. How embarrassing! Her face felt all hot. Her tummy felt like wiggly jelly. Probably her cheeks were all pink. Letting go of the hand, Patty again looked up. Her daddy was on the other side of her. She hid her face behind his Bible case. Patty was embarrassed.

But do you know that if you get embarrassed sometimes, that's OK? God has made our bodies in a wonderful way. The funny feeling in the tummy and the pink cheeks don't last very long.

Daddy smiled down at Patty and took her little hand in his big hand. Before long Patty was feeling fine—and so will you!—P.M.M.

Sugar and the Firecrackers

☀ *The people made so much noise. . . . It could be heard far away.* Ezra 3:13, ICB.

Big black Sugar, the Labrador dog, is a brave dog. If anyone he doesn't know comes near his home, he barks—a deep, doggy bark that warns, "You'd better not mess around here!" He also is a kind dog. He lets children climb on his strong back and play with his ears. But Sugar hates one thing: firecrackers.

Shooting off firecrackers, especially in some places, is against the law, even on the Fourth of July. But always a few people manage to get them. Sometimes they shoot them off on New Year's Eve or other times. And every time, Sugar goes wild. The noise scares him and hurts his ears. He races around his big yard and barks and barks and barks.

Sugar's family tries to help him. Although he is an outside dog, they let him come into the house when firecrackers are going off. He still shivers at the noise, but being inside with those he loves seems to help.

Do you ever hear noises that scare you? Funny thumps and bumps, often at night? I do. I've found out I can't sleep well until I know what they are.

One noise was a kind of low *bang-bang*. I found out it's just the gate to our chain link fence creaking when the wind blows. Then came a *thump bump*. Can you guess what it turned out to be? A squirrel leaping from the fence to the ground.

If you hear things that scare you, ask God to help you find out about them. It really helps. I know!—C.L.R.

Prisoner in the Granary

☀ *Do not worry about anything. But pray and ask God for everything you need. Phil. 4:6, ICB.*

Eddie walked slowly down the path toward the woods. He kicked a large stone as he went along, and whistled an off-key tune. As he rounded the sharp turn in the path, he heard a voice calling him. "Eddie, Eddie!"

"Yes, Mama!"

"Where are you going?"

"To the woods to hunt for acorns. I'll be back soon."

"Very well," called Mother, "but come back soon, and don't go anywhere else."

"OK, Mama. I'll be home in a little while."

Eddie often went to the woods. Mama didn't worry about him, because there were only about five acres of trees, and he could hardly get lost in that small space.

Before reaching the woods, he had to pass by the old granary. Eddie had never been inside. *I think I'll go in and see what's in there*, he said to himself. He forgot that Mama had told him not to go anywhere but the woods without telling her.

Arriving at the entrance of the sagging building, Eddie pushed hard on the old door. When he could not open it by pushing, he looked up. High above his head he noticed a small hook. Stretching on his tiptoes, he unhooked the door. It swung open on the rusty hinges with a loud creaking noise.

Around the edges of the room stood big metal barrels with labels on them. One of them read "Oats." Eddie soon became tired of looking, and decided to go to the woods. As he walked toward the door, he noticed a tall wooden barrel in the corner of the room.

I wonder what's in that barrel? thought Eddie. *It's different from the others.* Quickly he went to the corner, stood up on his toes, and tried to look inside. But his legs could not stretch far enough for him to see.

Suddenly he had an idea. He hooked his fingers over the top of the large barrel and pulled with all his might. Grunting and groaning, he lifted himself until he could see over the top. It looked very dark in the barrel, and he still couldn't see all the way to the bottom.

Lowering himself to the floor, Eddie rested while he thought about what to do. Then he noticed something he hadn't seen before. Over in one corner of the room sat a rickety old box.

Quickly he pulled the box close to the barrel and climbed up on it. He leaned over and looked inside. He bent his head a little, then a little more, and a little more, and a little more, until—"Oh!" Eddie screamed as he tumbled over the edge of the barrel and landed with a thud on something hard near the bottom.

He discovered that the barrel contained some old, hard salt. But now it held him prisoner, and he didn't know how to get out!

He reached his fingers over the edge of the barrel and pulled with all his strength, but strong as he thought himself to be, Eddie still couldn't pull himself up far enough to tumble over the side. What should he do? Oh, if only he had gone to the woods instead of coming to the granary!

Eddie began to think about his problem, and big tears ran down his cheeks. What if no one ever found him? What if the mouse Eddie thought he heard running on the other side of the room got into the barrel with him?

Then Eddie remembered that his Sabbath school teacher had told him that even when we don't do everything right, we can call for God to help us. Eddie knelt down in the bottom of the salt barrel and prayed that God would help him out of his trouble.

After Eddie prayed, he sat down in the bottom of the barrel, laid his head down on his bent knees, and went to sleep. When he awoke, his stomach felt very empty, and he knew it must be nearly time for dinner. Would Mama be looking for him?

Not many people used the lane near the granary, so Eddie knew it might be a long time before anyone found him. Over and over he called, but nobody came. Then, just when he wondered if God would answer his prayer, he heard someone singing.

The singing came from the lane.

That sounds like Arnie's singing, thought Eddie excitedly. Arnie helped Daddy with the farm chores sometimes, and he must be going to the back pasture for something.

"Arnie! Arnie! Help me, Arnie!" Eddie tugged at the edge of the barrel and tried to pull himself up, but he fell back into the barrel.

Suddenly the music stopped. He heard footsteps coming through the door, and felt himself being lifted out of the barrel.

"Well, well! What have we here?" Arnie said as he smiled down at Eddie. "How did you ever get in there?"

"Oh, thank you for helping me, Arnie. I tried to see what was in the barrel when—"

Eddie never got to finish his sentence, because at that moment Mama burst through the door.

Eddie ran happily into her arms.

"Oh, Mama," Eddie said. "I'm sorry I disobeyed, and I'm also glad that God answered my prayer for help."—M.K.S.

He That Is Slow to Anger

☀ *He that is slow to anger is better than the mighty. Prov. 16:32.*

Tommy had been teasing his little brother. After several warnings Mother scolded him and sent him to his room. She was annoyed with him when she went back to the kitchen to finish dinner.

After a few minutes Tommy called, "Mommy, can I p-l-e-a-s-e come out?"

"No, you may not!" Mother said firmly. "Don't ask me again! I'll let you know when your quiet time is up."

Linda, Tommy's 3-year-old sister, went over close to Mother, looked up, and said, "C'mere, Mommy," asking her to lean down. Usually when Mommy would do this, Linda would give her a big kiss. So Mother leaned down, but this time she didn't get a kiss. Instead, the little girl cupped her hands around her mother's ear and whispered, " 'He that is slow to anger is better than the mighty.' "

After Linda's special message, Mommy said thank You to Jesus for using her little girl to help her. She couldn't be angry anymore. She hugged Linda and gave her a big kiss and said, "Thank you, Linda, thank you very much! Mommy's not angry anymore."

Jesus gives wisdom to us all, whether we are large or small. — A.C.B.

Don't Be Afraid

I am not afraid in times of danger when I am surrounded by enemies, by evil men who trust in their riches and boast of their great wealth. Ps. 49:5, TEV.

Mike looked across the room. Dad was reading the paper. And he didn't seem scared by the things the newsman was saying on TV.

Dad put down the paper. "Something wrong, Mike?" he asked.

Mike went to sit on the stool by Dad's chair. "Well," he said, "the man on TV said awful things are happening to people these days." Mike moved closer to his dad. "He said some rich people are taking over everything."

Mike looked around the living room. He didn't want anyone to take their stuff. He liked their house and their things.

Dad set the paper aside and motioned to Mike to climb into his lap. "Don't be afraid," Dad said. "We'll be all right."

That made Mike feel better. So did sitting on Dad's lap. Still . . .

"On TV they talk about scary things," Dad said. "But we don't have to be afraid. Ever. Because God takes care of us."

"But if those people—"

"Ssssh," Dad said, hugging Mike close. "We belong to God. That's all we need to know."—N.C.P.

Hannah

Be kind to one another, tenderhearted, forgiving one another, just as God in Christ also forgave you. Eph. 4:32, NKJV.

Hannah was 9 years old. She lived with her mother and two sisters on the family farm. Even though Hannah was small, she had to work just like her sisters. And work was hard—picking cotton. Hannah would work in the cotton fields from early in the morning to late at night. With a sack tied to her little waist, Hannah would walk up and down the long rows of cotton in the hot sun. She pulled the cotton off the bushes and stuffed the white fluff into her bag. Hannah would stop once in a while to take a long, cool drink of water; then it was right back to picking cotton.

When her bag got filled, Hannah would drag it to the barn to be weighed. Each day Hannah prided herself that she picked the most cotton—oftentimes 200 pounds. And each day Hannah longed to hear her mother say, "I'm so proud of you, Hannah. You work so hard." But her mother never said those words to her.

Today Hannah is grown, and when she talks about her life on the farm she says, "Picking cotton was hard, hard work, and being out in the sun all day and never hearing thank you meant that many a night I went to my bed and cried. But," Hannah adds, "one thing I learned to do was to pray. I'd ask Jesus to help me be nice even though my mother didn't treat me with kindness like she treated my other sisters."

Hannah says this experience has helped her become a strong Christian, and she tries to be kind to everyone she meets. When someone does something for her, Hannah is quick to say thank you.

Everyone might not be kind to you, but Jesus wants you to be kind to everyone. That's being like Jesus.—C.B.T.

A Smile in Ivan's Heart

Whatever work you do, do your best. Eccl. 9:10, ICB.

Excitement bubbled out of Ivan. Daddy had said he was going to fix Mrs. McIntyre's floor, and Ivan could help.

Suddenly Ivan jumped up and nearly bumped into Mommy in his hurry to get to the front door. He had just seen Daddy pull into the driveway.

Ivan raced down the steps two at a time and shouted, "I'm ready to help! Can we go now?"

Daddy and Ivan climbed into the car with a collection of tools, nails, and wood. "I'm really pleased to have you come and work with me. I need someone who knows how important this job is," Daddy said.

Ivan's Sabbath school teacher had talked about Jesus' helpers. She read in the Bible where it said, "Whatever you did for one of the least of these brothers of mine, you did for me" (Matt. 25:40, NIV).

Jesus helped His mother at home and His father in the woodshop. It made Ivan smile to know that he could be a helper like Jesus.

At Mrs. McIntyre's house they marched up to the door. Ivan had a tool belt just like Daddy's. Ivan tried to stand as tall as could be. He wanted her to know that he had come to work too.

Ivan helped Daddy pull up the old flooring. They made sure that they removed all the splintery pieces of wood and each rusty, bent nail.

As they worked to get the spot ready for a new, strong board, Daddy said, "Ivan, you are so good at quickly bringing me the tools I need that I haven't had to stop and reach for anything."

Ivan smiled. "I try to guess what tool you'll need next," he said.

Mrs. McIntyre kept coming in and talking excitedly. "Oh, how wonderful it will be to have the room looking brand-new! I thought it would take a week. Should I order the new linoleum today?"

Daddy was pleased too. "That would be a good idea. Ivan and I will put it on the floor when it arrives."

Ivan nodded. He could hardly wait to come back and help lay the shiny, new linoleum.

When the new linoleum arrived, Daddy and Ivan returned and put it on the floor. When Daddy was all done, Ivan helped him gather up the tools and sweep the floor. "Daddy, the whole room looks brand-new!" he said proudly.

Mrs. McIntyre agreed. "I almost feel like I have a new house."

At supper Ivan told Mommy all about helping Daddy. "I had fun getting the tools for Daddy," he said thoughtfully, "and it made me feel happy when Mrs. McIntryĕ smiled so big when she saw the new floor."

"I know Jesus was smiling at His special helper too," Daddy said as he reached over and gave Ivan a big, warm hug. —L.R.

The Moose That Learned to Obey

☼ *If you are willing and obedient, you shall eat the good of the land. Isa. 1:19, RSV.*

A forest ranger in Denmark found a baby moose with a broken leg out in the woods. He named her Svea and brought her to his home until the leg was well. By this time Svea had become a very big moose. So the ranger took her back to live in the woods.

But Svea missed her human friends. One morning the ranger's daughter, Kirsten, heard a loud knock on the door. When she opened it, Svea bent her head so the girl could scratch it. Every morning before Kirsten went to school Svea came running from the edge of the forest. She'd stop and listen as Kirsten talked to her.

Later Svea found the nearby town. She loved to walk down the street. Children laughed as they followed her. She would not leave until Kirsten told her, "Go back to the woods, Svea."

The next day Svea smelled the bread baking in the bakery. She looked in the window until the baker gave her a loaf of fresh bread. Each day Svea would wait to get cookies or bread. The ranger took her in his truck far away, but in a few days she was back by the bakery window with the people she loved.

"We must take her far away to the zoo in the big city," the ranger said. When Svea arrived at the zoo, she looked all around the moose pen. Then with a big leap she jumped the nine-foot ditch, went to the parking lot, and put her nose down to love the children. After a while she willingly went back to the ditch, jumped across, and chose to stay where her friends had brought her. Svea, now obedient, never left her zoo home again.

Svea learned to be willing and obedient. Have you learned to put your toys away and come quickly when Mother or Daddy calls? You'll be happier if you obey right away. —E.E.L.

Where Is God?

You are all around me—in front and in back. Ps. 139:4, 5, ICB.

Let's fasten our seat belts so that we can get to the school on time for choir rehearsal," Mrs. Jones told her son, Louis, and their neighbor Sonja.

"Let's pray!" Louis said. He had already snapped the buckle on his red seat belt.

"We can't pray in the car!" Sonja shouted. "We're supposed to pray in church. Or we can pray at the dinner table or beside our bed but not in a car!"

"But God is everywhere!" Louis said, speaking a little louder than he usually did.

"Unh-unh!" Sonja protested.

"Mother!" Louis called for help.

"God does listen to our prayers in all the places you named, Sonja," Mother began, "but the Bible also says that He heard Jonah pray in the belly of a very big fish. And I know that God heard me pray in the driveway a few minutes ago when I couldn't find my car keys. So, children, I believe that God hears people pray wherever they are."

"I'll pray!" Sonja quickly volunteered.

"Thank you," mother said. "And then Louis will pray. God will hear you both."

Read about how God answered Jonah's prayer in Jonah 1:1 through Jonah 2:10. —F.J.C.

Walking and Praying

Lord, teach us to pray. Luke 11:1, NKJV.

Mommy, come and see the pretty, pretty snake." Standing by the open door in the dining room and looking down at the snake that had crawled into the house was 4-year-old Billy.

As Mommy got nearer to Billy, she quietly told him not to move, to stay right where he was standing. She could see that the pretty snake was a poisonous coral snake. And even though Mommy was walking and talking to Billy, she was also talking to Jesus. Very quietly she was praying to Jesus to send the snake away and not to let it bite Billy.

Slowly the snake moved away from Billy's feet and crawled under the bookshelf. Billy was not bitten. He had obeyed Mommy by not moving, and Jesus had answered Mommy's prayer. The snake was caught and killed.

Did Mommy have to get on her knees, bow her head, and close her eyes to pray? No, she didn't, but Jesus heard her prayer as she was walking toward Billy.

We can pray to Jesus when we walk, when we play, or when we are kneeling. He wants us to pray to Him. He likes it when we talk to Him. Praying to Jesus is like talking to your friend. You can talk to Jesus about anything. Jesus is always ready to listen. Get in the habit of praying to Jesus now. —C.B.T.

No Parachute

I'm tired of playing house. I wish there was something exciting to do."

Janie stared at the old shed in the backyard. Then one of her "bright" ideas came to her.

"I know just the thing, Mary. Do you remember when we were at the air show and saw those men in their parachutes sail through the air?"

"Yes, but . . ."

Before Mary could answer, Janie was talking again. "Come on. Let's take an umbrella and jump off the shed. If we open it, the umbrella will be just like a parachute, and we can sail through the air just like those men."

Mary looked doubtful. "It sounds like fun, but where do we get an umbrella? Do you have one?"

Janie looked thoughtful for a moment; then her eyes sparkled. "No, Mary, I don't have an umbrella, but your mother does. I know she wouldn't mind if we used it. We could get it back into the closet before she even knows we borrowed it."

Mary had been told not to play with Mother's umbrella. Daddy had brought it home from New York City, and Mother liked it very much. If it got broken, she would be very sad.

"Hurry!" Janie gave Mary a little push. "Your mother will be back from the store soon. We can have it all put back if we do it right now."

Mary ran quickly to get the umbrella while Janie placed a small ladder by the shed. When Mary and Janie stood on the ground, the shed did not look very high, but when they climbed onto the roof and looked down, it seemed like a long way to the ground.

Janie turned to Mary. "Since the umbrella belongs to your mother, I'll let you have the first turn," she said as she smiled sweetly.

"Oh, that's all right; you go first." Mary stepped carefully back from the edge of the roof. She pushed the umbrella toward Janie, but as Janie reached out her hand to grab it, she lost her balance, and suddenly she felt herself falling. Still holding on to the umbrella, she fell with a thud to the ground below.

"Oh, my foot hurts! Help me, Mary!"

Quickly Mary climbed down from the edge of the shed. Janie sat on the ground and held her foot and cried out in pain. Beside her lay the beautiful umbrella, all twisted and broken, with holes in the beautiful cloth.

Mary tried to help Janie stand up, but Janie's foot hurt so much that she could not get up. Just then Mother came home from the store. She helped Janie into the car and drove her to the doctor's office.

Janie did not have a broken foot, but it ached for a long time before she could walk on it again. While Janie's foot was healing, Mary got along without her allowance so she could pay for a new umbrella for Mother. —M.K.S.

Leaping Grandpas

☀ *Then the lame shall leap like a deer. Isa. 35:6, NKJV.*

Josh and Jimmy loved to visit Grandpa. His backyard was full of pretty flowers and bushes. The perfect place to play games! Grandpa was old, and he couldn't walk very well without a wooden cane to lean on, but he would sit on the patio and watch while the boys played.

One day after a good game of tag, Jimmy picked up a large stick. "This is the best stick in the world." he said.

"No, it's not." Josh replied. "I can find a better stick than yours." He ran down the path to look for a stick. Suddenly he saw Grandpa's walking cane leaning against his chair. It was strong and sturdy, much better than Jimmy's stick. The old man had fallen asleep.

Josh crept over to the chair and took Grandpa's cane. He and Jimmy had fun with it hitting rocks up in the air. "This is a better stick!" Jimmy exclaimed.

Suddenly they heard a thud! Grandpa had awakened and tried to walk without his cane. He had fallen to the ground. Both boys ran to help him up.

"Oh, Grandpa, I'm so sorry!" Josh said.

"You're forgiven," Grandpa said. "But you must never take my cane again. My legs are not strong like yours. One day Jesus is coming to take us to heaven. Then He will give me strong legs, and then I will run, jump, and leap all over heaven. I will be able to play games with you and Jimmy then."

Name some other things that Grandpa and Josh will be able to do in heaven that they can't do now. —C.B.E.

The Burr Haircut

✺ Be sure your sin will find you out. Num. 32:23.

Joyce tossed her long golden curls back over her shoulder. "Harry Lee, may I play with you?" she asked. Their mothers were both busy with fall cleaning inside the church school.

"Can you do this?" teased Harry Lee as he pressed a big fistful of cockleburs firmly onto the top of his head.

"Don't do that! You'll never get them out," warned Joyce.

"Sure I can—watch me." Harry pulled the sticky burrs out of his short red hair without it hurting a bit. "See, it's easy," he said. "Try it."

Joyce picked a handful of the burrs and placed them very gently on top of her head. She remembered how much it hurt when Mother combed tangles out of her hair.

"Not like that," scoffed Harry Lee. "Like this!" He pounded a bunch into his hair with a smart smack.

He thinks he's so smart, Joyce said to herself. *I'll show him who's smart!* She packed the burrs down until even Harry Lee said that it was enough. Then she tried to take them out. Uh-oh. Stuck tight—*no way would they come out!*

She pulled and pulled until the tears came to her eyes. She couldn't tell Mother. Mother would scold her and pull even harder. What *could* she do?

Joyce got an idea—she would use those scissors Mom kept in the glove compartment of the car. She ran to the car and looked at herself in the mirror. "I'm going to have burrs on my head for the rest of my life," she wailed.

Joyce knew that she was not supposed to touch those scissors, and she had been punished before for cutting her brother's hair. But this was an emergency!

She slipped the shiny scissors out and began very carefully to cut away the burrs. *Snip, snip, snip* went the scissors. "Kids-can't-cut-hair; kids-can't-cut-hair," they seemed to say. But Joyce was very careful and patient, taking only little pieces of hair with each snip.

143

At last she could see no more burrs in the mirror. And, wonder of wonders, her hair seemed to be all there in spite of what lay on the car seat tangled with the burrs. Mother would never know. She felt much better, and ran off to play.

It was late when they got home that night, and Joyce went straight to bed. In the morning when Mother took the barrettes out of Joyce's hair to brush her hair for school, what a surprise! A big, long chunk of Joyce's hair fell off into Mother's hand. The barrette had held it in place all that time.

When Mom finished brushing Joyce's hair, she let her look in the mirror. "Want to tell me where you got that ugly-looking haircut?" asked Mom.

"That dumb Harry Lee," sobbed Joyce. And she told Mom the whole sad story. "Are you going to punish me?" she asked.

"No," said Mom. "You have punished yourself. You'll have to wear those weird-looking bangs wherever you go until your hair grows out."

For a long time whenever Joyce looked in the mirror she was reminded that really smart kids don't listen when dumb kids tell them what to do. —B.V.

Mushroom "Manna"

☀ *He sent them food to the full.* Ps. 78:25, NKJV.

Do you know about the pioneers? They were people who came to this country a long time ago. When they arrived, they had no homes and no jobs. They wanted to start a new life. They had to work very hard to build houses out of logs and to feed their families.

I want to tell you about some modern-day pioneers—the Fulton family. They had just moved out West. They had no money, and Dad had no job. Every meal it was the same thing—bread, margarine, and honey. They worked hard to build a log cabin, cutting trees and putting the logs together. But they were a happy family and thankful for God's blessings.

One day after family worship, Dad went out to cut wood. Suddenly Dad threw down the chain saw and gave a loud yell. Mom came running as she saw Dad hopping around. "Come quickly!" Dad yelled. Everyone was sure Dad was hurt badly.

As Mom and the three children got closer, they saw something on the ground. Mushrooms! One hundred large, nonpoisonous mushrooms—just like the ones they had picked back in Maryland! "Whoopie!" they yelled. Now they had food to last until money would come in the mail the next week.

When Mr. Fulton's dad heard the story, he didn't believe it. He wanted proof. So he prayed while Mr. Fulton went to search for more mushrooms. God let him find just one mushroom. Then Mr. Fulton's dad believed. Every spring since then, his dad has looked in the same spot for mushrooms, but he has never found them.

I believe God sent those mushrooms, don't you?—P.H.

A Special
Father's Day Gift

Go watch the ants. . . . Watch what they do and be wise. Prov. 6:6, ICB.

Father's Day is right around the corner, Mom," Kent said, "and we don't have enough money to buy Daddy even a tie."

Kent sounded so glum that Mom volunteered to give her children a few dollars. But Kent said, "No thanks, Mom, that would be like Dad buying his own gift."

Kent and his brothers had $1.78, so they bowed their heads and asked Jesus to help them decide what to do with it. After prayer, Mattias said excitedly, "Let's do chores for Dad's gift! They bought wrapping paper, a special pen, and yarn to make a coupon book that named the jobs they would do for Dad.

Kent said, "Let's each put our jobs on separate coupons. Some of the jobs they decided to do were: wash the car; clean the driveway; shine the family's shoes. The coupon book grew and grew.

They put the book into a small box and wrapped it, and then put it in another box, and that box into another, until it was in a very large fancy box.

Father's Day finally arrived. Dad laughed harder and harder as he opened all the boxes. Then, looking at the coupon book, he said, "Wise decision. How did you boys know what I needed most? Thanks; this is better than any tie or aftershave lotion."

The boys looked at each other and smiled.

Do you need Jesus to help you?—A.C.B.

Grandma, Go Home

☀ *While they were there [Mary and Joseph at Bethlehem], the time came for the baby to be born. Luke 2:6, NIV.*

Two-year-old Julie lived with her mother and father in a happy, cozy home. One day Mother said, "Guess what, Julie? Grandma is coming to stay with us."

Julie clapped her hands. Grandma was a fun person, and Julie loved her.

Mother went on. "Grandma is going to stay a few days and take care of you and Daddy, who is her little boy all grown up. I'm going to the hospital, and when I come back, I hope that I will have a wonderful present—your own little sister or brother."

Julie thought and thought. Her own little sister or brother? It must be nice, because Mother looked very, very happy.

Soon Mother went away, and Grandma came. Always before, Julie liked having Grandma there. This time she said, "Grandma, go home."

Grandma felt terrible. So did Julie's father.

"Grandma, go home." Julie said it over and over. But Grandma couldn't go home. Her son needed her and so would Julie's mother and the new baby when they came home.

Then Mother and baby Kelly came home. Julie danced up and down. She looked at her little sister. She looked at Mother. She ran to Grandma and climbed into her lap. "Grandma, no go home! Mommy bring baby Kelly. Grandma, no go home. Grandma stay with Julie."

At last Grandma and Julie's parents understood that the little girl had thought her mother wouldn't come home as long as Grandma stayed! How happy they all were to get things worked out!

Can you remember a time when either Mommy or Daddy had to be gone for a while and you felt afraid that they might not come back?—C.L.R.

The Blessing

Love your enemies; do good to those who hate you; bless those who curse you; pray for those who treat you spitefully. Luke 6:27, 28, REB.

All my relatives were coming to my aunt's house in the city for Thanksgiving, but I got to stay overnight the day before to help her make the dessert.

We baked two pumpkin pies and two apple pies. Then we set them, steaming hot, on the wide porch railing to cool.

"Is that yummy smell making your tummy do somersaults?" Tia Alma asked.

"Sure is," I laughed.

"Mine too. I have just the thing for us." Tia Alma made apple-cinnamon oatmeal. We ate it while the pies cooled. I went to check them while my aunt cleaned up. What I saw made me freeze in the doorway.

Finally I found my voice. "Tia, Tia!" I cried. "A man took our pies."

She dashed out. "What man? Where? Did you see him?" Her head darted back and forth.

"Yes, it was the homeless man whom Tio Hector calls Scummy." Tia Alma clucked her tongue.

"Sorry," I said, looking down.

Tia Alma hugged me close. "God bless him," she said.

" 'God bless him'?" I repeated. "He stole from us, Tia. That's wrong!"

"So is hunger, Elena." She hugged me close in the chilly air. "Our family won't starve without those pies. Anyone hungry enough to steal someone's Thanksgiving dessert needs a blessing more than we need pies."

I shivered. Then I thought of my full tummy and Tia Alma's cozy kitchen, and suddenly I felt warm.

"God bless him," I whispered. I could see my breath.

Tia Alma smiled, and we went inside. —V.L.K.

Give to Others

☀ *Give to others, and God will give to you. Luke 6:38, TEV.*

Terry pressed her finger hard on the colored ribbon while Mother tied the bow. The package was pretty, wrapped in silvery paper and a bright blue bow.

Terry looked at the other presents. "Mother," she said, "why are we giving Mrs. Harper a party? She's not a relative of ours."

Mother looked up. "Why are you asking me a question like that?"

"Sally said we were going to end up in the poorhouse because you're always giving things away."

Mother laughed. "I suppose Sally heard that from her mother. Do you even know what a poorhouse is?"

Terry frowned. "No, but it sounded bad."

"Well, don't worry about it," Mother said. "Nothing like that is going to happen to us."

"But Mother, you do keep giving things away. Last year you gave Mrs. Walker a winter coat."

Mother smiled. "Mrs. Walker needed a coat, and I had two."

"But you gave her your better one."

Mother fluffed up the bow. "God tells us to give to others. And He tells us that if we do, He will give to us."

Terry looked around at their house. The things in it weren't new and shiny like the things in Sally's house, but Terry liked it better. Mother didn't wear fancy clothes and drive a new car like Sally's mother did. But then Sally's mother was never home, and she didn't even like for Sally to hug her because it messed up her fine clothes.

Terry went around the table and gave Mother a big hug. "I'm glad *you're* my mother," she said.

Mother hugged her back. "I'm glad too." —N.C.P.

A Birthday Each Week

☀ *Remember the sabbath day. Ex. 20:8.*

Do you like birthdays?

Mariyan could not wait until her birthday. She was going to be 3 years old. Her mommy, daddy, and big brother, Artie, were going to have a party for her—a zoo party! She would have an elephant cake and monkey peanuts, and all her friends would get their faces painted to look like their favorite zoo animal. Oh, what a fun time it would be!

"Mommy, I want every day to be my birthday."

"Mariyan," Mommy said, "your birthday comes only once a year. After your zoo party is over, you will have to wait until next year to have another birthday."

But there is a special day that we can remember each week, and it is sort of like a birthday. It is the Sabbath day. Every week Jesus sends the Sabbath to us. On the Sabbath we can do fun things like go to Sabbath school, or have lunch at a friend's house, or walk or ride with Mommy and Daddy. It's a day when we can think about how much Jesus loves us.

I'm glad that Jesus made the Sabbath day for us to remember each week. Aren't you? It's almost like having a birthday party every week.

Maybe you can talk with Mommy or Daddy and plan what you can do together to have a happy Sabbath this week. —M.M.M.

I Wish I Could Be

☀ *Even a child is known by his actions, by whether his conduct is pure and right. Prov. 20:11, NIV.*

Jerry was making a list. Not a shopping or spelling or birthday list, but a different kind of list. He sang a song he had made up while he wrote: "Oh, I wish I could be, someone else, not me."

He finished his list and showed it to his mother. "This is a list of what I'd like to be instead of me."

1. an astronaut
2. Billy Henry
3. a horse
4. Mr. Donaldson
5. Sally Taylor

"Why do you want to be anyone or anything different than yourself?" Mom asked.

"Well, astronauts get to fly close to heaven, where God lives. Billy Henry has a new football. A horse doesn't have to go to school; it just runs around in the sunshine. Mr. Donaldson's a banker and lives in a swell place with a pool." He stopped. "I almost didn't put Sally Taylor down, but she lives in the country by a frog pond. I'd make a terrible girl, though."

"Hmmmm." Mom looked at the list. "Astronauts have to be away from home a lot and probably don't get many warm, homemade cookies. The reason Billy got a new football is because they're moving, and he hates to go. A horse? Think you'd like living in a barn with just hay for every meal?" Jerry giggled, but Mom went on. "The Donaldsons' daughter is sick, and they're moving too. Sally can't get to town for Sabbath school. Still want to be one of them?"

"Oh, I don't want to be anyone else, just me!" Jerry sang. It was his new song. —C.L.R.

Condensed from *Our Little Friend,* May 27, 1989.

They Said, "Thank You"

In everything give thanks; for this is the will of God in Christ Jesus for you. 1 Thess. 5:18, NKJV.

Walking down the road, a man saw a little dove lying in the grass. It was hurt. He picked it up and took it home. Carefully he put it in a cage and gave it fresh water to drink and seeds and berries to eat. Soon it could move around.

After eight days of good care, the dove seemed well and strong. Carrying the cage to the top of a hill, the man opened the door. Right away the dove flew out and into the woods.

A week later the man went back to the same place and sat on a rock. Suddenly a little bird flew to him and sat on his arm. He knew it was the same little dove. He felt that the little bird had stopped to tell him, "Thank you for helping me get well."

Another man was hiking through tall grass when he heard a crying sound. He turned around and saw a wildcat walking toward him. Afraid, because wildcats bite people, the man almost ran away. Then he saw that the wildcat's mouth looked swollen and sore.

The man knelt down and took the wildcat's head in his hands. Gently he opened the swollen mouth. One of the wildcat's sharp teeth stuck through the animal's tongue. The tooth held the tongue fast so that the animal couldn't eat or drink. Carefully the man pulled the tongue loose, though he knew it hurt the wildcat a lot. But the wildcat didn't move. When he finished, the man patted the animal, and the wildcat leaned against him and meowed as if to say "Thank you for helping me." Then it went to the stream to get water.

Both the dove and the wildcat remembered to say thank you in their own way. Do you thank Mother and Daddy for the good food and clothes they give you? or your friends when they do nice things? Do you thank Jesus for the flowers and birds? Remember to say thank you. —E.E.L.

Katherine's Kitten

Give thanks to him and bless his name. Ps. 100:4, NEB.

All that Katherine could think about was getting a kitten. She prayed, "Dear Jesus, please give me a kitten. I want it to be all gray. *Not black-and-white, not calico, but gray.*"

Then Katherine got a little box, put it under her bed, and put a soft cloth in it. She got a dish for milk and placed it alongside the box. She told her mother, "Mama, Jesus is going to send me a little kitten. It's going to be all gray, and I'm going to name it Chubby."

"Oh," Mother said, "why don't you ask Jesus for something else? We don't want any cats."

"Please, *pretty please!*" Katherine begged. She wanted that kitten more than anything else in the world. But Mother hoped Katherine would forget all about the kitten.

Soon after, Katherine and Mother were traveling along a country road when suddenly Katherine shouted, "Look, Mama! There it is! My kitten!" It was all gray—just the color kitten Katherine had asked for.

As Katherine cuddled the soft, fluffy kitten in her arms, a lady came up to her and said, "You may have him if you like."

"Goodie!" Katherine squealed.

When Mother saw the wishful look in Katherine's eyes she said, "Yes, let's name him Chubby."

When Katherine got home, she put Chubby in his box. But she forgot to do something very important. Can you guess what it was? She should have gotten on her knees and thanked Jesus for sending her the kitten. Do you remember to thank Jesus when He answers *your* prayers?—P.H.

Let's Make Smiley Faces!

☼ *He has sent me to comfort all those who are sad. Isa. 61:2, ICB.*

Billy stretched his neck as far as he could so he could get the last look at his father driving that shiny blue car. After a day in the Elyria, Ohio, park, Billy's friends—two carloads of them—were going back to Cleveland, Ohio.

Billy yawned. He rolled up the car window and laid his head in his mother's lap. But before he could get comfortable, Billy felt himself crashing against the front seat. He heard screaming. Something scratched his face.

"Mother!" Billy cried.

"We're all right, Billy," Mother said. "Another car smashed into our car, but Jesus has kept us safe."

Mother helped Billy sit up. She picked little pieces of the glass window out of his black hair and off his green T-shirt. Daddy lifted Billy over the front seat and out of the door, because the car door next to where Billy had been sitting was smashed in.

Whir! Whir! Whir! An ambulance came to take Billy and his mother to the hospital to be examined. "You're a very lucky little boy," the driver told Billy as they walked toward the ambulance. The driver bent down and rolled a tire out of their path. He looked around at the hubcaps and fenders and car mirrors that were scattered beside the road. "I'm glad that you have just a few bruises, Billy," the driver said.

That night Billy lay in his bed, thinking. *Thank You, Jesus, for keeping me safe. I wish that I could teach people to trust You to help them when they're sad. I want to help people like the drunk driver who smashed into our car.* "I want to be a minister!" Billy said it so loudly that he scared himself!

That December Billy was baptized. "Oh!" he giggled softly when the cold water in the baptismal pool filled the legs of his knickers. Splash! the water rippled when Pastor Laurence dipped Billy beneath the water.

Billy became a minister when he grew up, and he has worked hard to make his wish come true. He has baptized more than 5,000 people and has taught them to trust Jesus to help them when they're sad.

Can you show me how a sad person's face looks? How can you help a sad person wear a smiley face?

[Note to parents. Elder William C. Scales is the Ministerial Association director for the North American Division.]—F.J.C.

Moving Day

✳ O my God, make haste to help me! Ps. 71:12, NKJV.

The moving van had pulled in front of the Martin house, bringing their furniture. Mother told the children that she did not want them to get in the way of the men when they started carrying the boxes and furniture into the house. The three Martin children were excited. The family's furniture had finally come.

All day the house had been noisy and busy with excitement. The front door was open wide, and the men had been walking back and forth from the house to the moving van as they brought in boxes of books, boxes of toys, and boxes of dishes. There were lots of boxes to take into the house. Some of the boxes were taken to the bedrooms, some to the living room, some to the dining room. The moving men brought in the piano and put it in the living room. They brought the beds in and took them upstairs to the bedrooms. The table and chairs were taken to the kitchen.

Mother was busy making sure that the boxes and furniture were going to the right rooms when all of a sudden Mother remembered that she hadn't seen Little Brother or Dog for a long time. Mother stopped putting away dishes and glasses, and started looking for Little Brother.

"Where is Little Brother?" Mother wondered out loud. Mother looked upstairs in the bedrooms. No Little Brother. She looked in the bathroom. No Little Brother. She looked outside in the backyard. No Little Brother. Mother looked in the front yard. No Little Brother.

Mother said to the men who were helping the family move into their new house, "Have you seen my little boy and our dog? I can't find them anywhere."

The moving men said that they hadn't seen her little boy or the dog.

Mother was upset. Where could they be? Mother called the other two children and told them that Little Brother and Dog were lost. Mrs. Nelson, the neighbor, came to the house, and Mother told her about Little Brother and Dog—that she could not find them. Mother began to cry. Mrs. Nelson put her hand on Mother's arm and told her that Little Brother would be found.

As they were sitting in the living room looking very sad, into the living room walked Little Brother and Dog. Oh, how happy everyone was!

"Where were you?" asked Mother. "We were all so very, very worried. Where have you been?"

Little Brother said, "Mommy, you said not to get in the way of the moving men, so I took Dog and went to my secret hiding place."

"And where was that?" asked Mother. "Show me."

Little Brother took Mother to the kitchen, opened the cabinet door under the sink, and showed her where he and Dog had been all the time they were looking for them. Mommy hugged Little Brother and patted Dog. She said, "You had us all frightened, but I'm glad you were safe."—C.B.T.

The Best Gift

Every good gift and every perfect gift is from above and comes down from the Father. James 1:17, NKJV.

It was Trina's birthday. Mommy and Daddy surprised her with a pink birthday cake. Daddy even blew up balloons and hung them from the ceiling. Grandma and Grandpa bought Trina a beautiful doll, and Big Brother helped Daddy build Trina a dollhouse.

After opening her presents and eating a piece of cake, Trina said, "This is the best birthday ever. Thank you, Mommy and Daddy. Thank you, Grandma and Grandpa. Thank you, Big Brother."

"You are welcome," Daddy said. "But have you thanked Jesus for the presents He gave you?"

"What did Jesus give me?" Trina asked.

"He sent an angel to watch over you all year and keep you safe. He gave you sunshine to play in, good food to eat, and a warm house to live in."

"Oh," said Trina. "I didn't think of that. But He gives me those presents every day, not just on my birthday."

"You're right," Grandpa laughed. "Every day is like a birthday with Jesus. Why don't we make a list of presents that we are grateful for and then kneel down and thank Him?"

What has Jesus given *you* that you are thankful for?—C.B.E.

Mercy's Cabin

Everyone who hears these words of mine and puts them into practice is like a wise man who built his house on the rock. Matt. 7:24, NIV.

Mercy's family crossed the ocean on a big ship to join the other Pilgrim settlers in America. They stayed with the Eatons while Papa built their cabin.

Moving day came at last. Mercy hugged her doll Charity. "We're going to a real home, a real home, a real home!" she sang. Mercy's long braids bounced under her calico bonnet as she skipped.

Mercy's eyes lit up when she saw the cabin. There were hay-stuffed mattresses for her and Mama and Papa and a small rocking cradle for baby Lucas.

The hearth was warm and welcoming. A black cooking kettle hung over the fire. In the heart of the cabin stood a long oak table with benches for eating, praying, working, or talking. Two boards on the wall made a sturdy cupboard.

Mama set baby Lucas in his cradle and unpacked their belongings. She stacked dishes and refolded clothing.

Mrs. Eaton gave Mama a new straw broom and flour and yams for the pantry. Papa brought in a freshly killed pheasant. While dinner was cooking, Mama put quilts over the mattresses.

Mercy felt comfortable and cozy. "Look, Charity," she said, "now our home is complete."

Baby Lucas cooed.

"It's not complete yet," Papa said.

Mercy was surprised. "What's missing, Papa?"

Papa searched every corner of the cabin. Finally he held a big black Book in his strong, worn hands.

"Is that our Holy Bible?" Mercy asked.

"Yes," Papa answered. He set the book in the center of the table.

"Now," Mercy said, "our home is complete." — V.L.K.

A Better Helper

☀ *You made me in an amazing and wonderful way. Ps. 139:14, ICB.*

"Toys!" Charlie yelled when he saw his mother looking through a catalog. Rushing to where she was sitting on the carpet, he asked, "What's that?" Charlie pointed to the picture that his mother had marked with a red X.

"That's a wonderful bread machine, Charlie," Mother replied. She read the advertisement to him: "Set the timer, mix the bread before bedtime, and wake up in the morning smelling fresh bread." Mother sniffed the air in spite of herself.

Sighing, she closed the catalog and looked up at Charlie. "Help me stand up, please," she said. Holding her hands, Charlie dug his sneakers into the carpet. He tightened his leg muscles and his arm muscles, and pulled. "Unh!" Charlie groaned as Mother, laughing, stood straight up.

"Thank you, Charlie," she said, patting him on his shiny black, soft, curly hair. "You're quite a machine yourself."

"I am?" Charlie asked, his brown eyes shining.

"You surely are!" Mother exclaimed. "You're strong and smart. You help me mix the bread batter. You help knead the dough with your fingers. And you always make sure to hand me the potholders when it's time to take the hot pans of bread out of the oven."

Mother paused and put her forefinger on her lips. Charlie knew she was thinking. "You know, Charlie, I can't afford that bread machine, but I don't need it. Do you know why?" Then, quickly gathering Charlie in her arms, she answered for him, "Because I've got a wonderfully made little boy named Charlie."

How do you help other people?

Let's thank God for giving us wonderful bodies. —F.J.C.

"Well, Mommy, You See . . ."

☀ *You shall not give false testimony. Ex 20:16, NIV.*

Rhonda," Mother asked, "why are you late coming from school?"

With her forehead wrinkled like one of Daddy's old boots, Rhonda said, "Well, Mommy, you see . . . there was a big wreck, and a little girl got hit 'cause the traffic lady was sitting down resting."

"Oh, dear," Mother said as she pretended to look worried. "We better go see if the ambulance has come to help the poor little girl."

Rhonda got worried and said, "I'm sure she's OK. You don't have to worry . . ."

But Mother got her sweater and took Rhonda by the hand, saying, "Come, let's go see if she's all right."

When they got to the street where the accident was supposed to have happened, no one was there. "Let's go to the school," Mother said. On the way to school, with tears meeting under her chin, Rhonda said, "We don't need to go, Mommy."

By the time they reached the school, Rhonda was crying great big tears.

"Rhonda," Mommy said, "you must remember that Jesus wants us always to tell the truth."

"I'm sorry, Mommy, I really am! There wasn't any accident. I didn't tell the truth. Please, Mommy, I promise, I won't do that anymore!"— A.C.B.

Keep Your Eyes Open

Open my eyes to see wonderful things. Ps. 119:18, TLB.

Gary, Loren," Dad called. "Let's go for a walk in the woods."

"Put your jackets on, guys," Mom reminded. The leaves had already turned from green to gold, orange, and brown. The fall breezes could get cool on bare arms.

Mom, Dad, and the boys hiked along a trail almost hidden by leaves. A stream trickled beside the path.

"Keep your eyes open, boys," Mom encouraged. "See what you can find special."

Dad was first to see the raccoon footprints by the stream. Mom found bright-yellow flowers called goldenrods. Loren spotted a deer running into the woods in the distance.

Sadly Gary said, "I can't find anything special."

"Keep your eyes open, Gary," cheered Mom. "You'll find something."

Gary decided that he would walk a few steps ahead of the others. He looked up into the trees. Gary looked in the bushes. He looked down on the ground. Suddenly from the edge of the path a bird exploded into the air. Gary jumped in surprise.

"What was that?" Mom and Dad exclaimed almost at the same time.

"I know," said Gary. "It's in the book about birds that you just read to us, Mom."

As soon as the family got home, Gary ran to get the book Mom had read from earlier in the week.

"It was a woodcock," Mom announced to the rest of the family. The boys had learned that a woodcock sits very still even if you come near. When almost stepped on, the woodcock bursts into the air. What a wonderful Sabbath surprise for the whole family!

The next time you take a walk, keep your eyes open. God has filled the outdoors with wonderful surprises!—P.M.M.

Deep Water

He reached down from on high and took hold of me; he drew me out of deep waters. 2 Sam. 22:17, NIV.

Dan took swimming lessons for a few times, then moved to a place where they didn't have a pool. It didn't matter, though, for close by was the whole Pacific Ocean.

"Son," Dad told him, "swimming in an ocean is nothing like swimming in a pool. There are no sides to grab on to if you get tired. Never ever swim out a long way. Go out and swim back toward shore, and never ever swim alone. You are going to be in major trouble if I catch you anywhere near the ocean unless your mother is with you if I can't be. Right?"

"Right." Dan secretly didn't know how he felt about water that looked like it went on until it got all mixed up with the sky.

One day during a family picnic Dan raced out onto the pier that went into the ocean.

"Careful!" Dad shouted, but Dan heard him too late. He slipped on a wet spot. His arms went wild, but he couldn't balance. Splat! Right into the deep, deep water he fell. He went down so far that his lungs felt like they would explode if he couldn't have air soon. Finally he shot back up to the top. Before he could sink again, Dad's strong arms reached down from the pier, grabbed him, and pulled him out of danger.

Dan lay gasping on the warm planks, dizzy and glad Dad had been there.

At family worship that night, Dad and Mom gave thanks to God for His loving care that saves us from sin, just as Dad saved Dan. — C.L.R.

The Horse That Wouldn't Quit

☀ *I can do all things through Christ who strengthens me. Phil. 4:13, NKJV.*

Old Nell had been a good horse. Now she was too old to work. She could hardly walk, so the farmer put her in a field with grass to eat. One day he couldn't find her.

Where could she be? he wondered. Then he remembered a big hole that had once had water in it. He looked. Yes, Old Nell had fallen to the bottom. He saw her brown back. When he called her name, she answered with a whinny.

"Too bad," said the farmer. "Maybe she broke her leg when she fell. That hole's deep. I need help to get her out. Maybe I should just fill it up and bury Old Nell at the same time."

The farmer got a shovel and began throwing dirt on the horse. He felt ashamed as he remembered the many years that Old Nell had worked hard. So he stood far back from the hole where he couldn't see the horse as he shoveled the dirt. He hoped she wouldn't suffer long.

When Old Nell felt the dirt hit her back, she shook it off. Her legs weren't broken, though they were very stiff and sore. She stomped on the dirt. More dirt fell. She shook it off too. Her legs hurt, but she kept stepping on the dirt. Without water or food, she became tired. Still she didn't stop shaking the dirt off her back and stomping on it. She wouldn't quit. The farmer, who hated himself for being so unkind, shoveled faster to get it over with. Old Nell worked hard too. The dirt got higher and higher in the hole.

Finally the farmer stopped to rest. Suddenly he saw a horse's head coming out of the hole. While he watched, Old Nell slowly crawled out and went to her favorite place under the trees.

Sometimes your mother asks you to work—clean your room or wipe the dishes. Do you keep on working even when it's hard? Be like Old Nell. Don't quit. Keep trying until you finish your job. —E.E.L.

Weeding Out Sin

We should bear fruit to God. Rom. 7:4, NKJV.

Six-year-old Aaron loved to help Daddy in the garden. One day Daddy showed Aaron some prickly plants growing among the spinach. "This is a weed," Daddy told him. "We do not want weeds in our garden."

"Why?" Aaron wanted to know.

"Weeds grow very quickly," Daddy explained. "They multiply and spread. They gobble up the food and water in the soil that our vegetables need to grow. They also shade the vegetables and keep them from getting the sunshine they need."

Aaron knelt beside Daddy and began pulling the weeds. Some of the weeds were easy to pull, but others had strong roots. Aaron pulled and pulled on one weed, but it would not come out of the ground. Daddy reached over and helped him pull the weed. It popped right out and sprayed them both with dirt.

"These weeds are like sin in the heart," Daddy said as he wiped the dirt off Aaron's face. "One little sin grows and grows until it crowds out the good things."

"Do you mean our hearts are like a garden?" Aaron asked.

Daddy laughed. "Yes. The bad things we say and do are like weeds. I can't pull even one sin out of my heart, but Jesus is stronger than both of us. He can pull up the mean weeds. All we have to do is ask Him. Then we must water our little heart garden with Bible verses and prayers. Only then can we grow and bear good fruit."

What kind of weeds do you have in your heart? How can you get them out?—C.B.E.

Wait Awhile

☀ *The dead in Christ will rise first. 1 Thess. 4:16, NIV.*

The doctor told Edwina that her mother had cancer.

"Will my mommy be all right?" Edwina asked the doctor.

"Yes. She will need an operation to take the cancer out, and after that she should be fine," explained the doctor.

"Mommy, I hope you'll be all right," said Edwina.

"I will, honey. Nothing can separate us from God's love," her mother said. "God's love surrounds us, and we have no need to fear."

"Mommy, I want to ask Jesus to heal you."

"OK, honey. Remember, Jesus knows what's best for Mommy. Jesus always answers our prayers."

Edwina prayed, "Jesus, please heal my mommy, if You want to. Thank You. Amen. "

Edwina's mommy's operation went fine. She was feeling stronger—strong enough to ride a long way to camp meeting.

Mommy was rubbing her stomach one day, and Edwina noticed.

"Mommy, is your tummy OK?"

"I just have lots of gas. That's what happens after surgery."

"Oh, may I rub your tummy, Mommy?"

"Sure! Ummm, that feels so good! I love you, Edwina."

"I love you, Mommy."

Mommy's stomach pains didn't go away. Her stomach got bigger and bigger. When they got back from camp meeting, Mommy went to the doctor. He found cancer in her stomach, too.

"Mommy, I'm scared. You are so sick."

"Mommy loves Jesus, Edwina. Everything is going to be all right."

Mommy got worse. She died.

Jesus always answers our prayers. Sometimes Jesus says yes; sometimes, no; sometimes, wait awhile. Edwina will have to wait awhile for her mother to be healed, but because her mother loved Jesus, she will rise again when Jesus comes, and she will have a new body. —E.G.N.

Daddy Knows Everything!

The righteous are as bold as a lion. Prov. 28:1, NASB.

Esther and her sister Ellen skipped along the hallway of the Piccadilly Circus train station. They had been to the New Gallery Centre Church in London.

"Let's wait for Mother and Daddy," 5-year-old Esther said. The girls stepped out of the way of the crowd and stood next to a white-haired lady.

"Good afternoon," Ellen said.

"Good afternoon," the lady answered. "You girls look very lovely in your frilly pink dresses."

"Thank you!" the girls said. Then they talked about the lovely day.

"I see my girls have made a new friend," Daddy said when he came up. He tugged their long black ponytails and smiled at the lady.

"Your daughters do know how to make friends," the lady said.

"And my daddy knows everything—except when Jesus is going to come again!" Esther said cheerfully.

"Is Jesus coming again?" the lady asked.

"That is what Jesus promised," Daddy explained.

Ellen handed the lady a Voice of Prophecy Bible study card. "Mail this card, and you'll learn all about Jesus' promise."

"Oh, thank you!" the lady said.

"All aboard for Charing Cross!" the engineer called out as the engine chugged into the station yard.

Mother and the girls waved goodbye. Daddy talked about Jesus with the lady for a few more minutes before getting into the passenger car. As Daddy neared his family's seat, he heard Esther tell the man across the aisle, "My daddy knows everything—except when Jesus is going to come again!"

"Is Jesus coming again?" the man asked, peering over his black-rimmed glasses.

Daddy smiled and began to explain about the promise Jesus made long ago.

Today Esther Ramharacksing Knott is a pastor for the Sligo church near Washington, D.C. She says that telling people about Jesus when she was a little girl taught her to be bold for Him.

Do you tell people about Jesus?

Jesus can help you be bold like little Esther was. —F.J.C.

A Little Child Shall Lead Them

✺ *The wolf also shall dwell with the lamb, the leopard shall lie down with the young goat . . . and a little child shall lead them.* Isa. 11:6, NKJV.

Plop! The monkey jumped onto the dog's back. He looked in the dog's ears, picked in his fur, and then . . . looked in his mouth. And the dog just lay there as if he knew that the monkey would not hurt him. And the monkey seemed to know that the dog was not going to hurt him. So the two animals sat side by side while the family finished singing songs and praying to Jesus in family worship.

Wouldn't that be nice if all animals could play together like the dog and the monkey?

But that wasn't the way it was with Babs and Baby, the two kittens that had come to live at the Smiths' house. As the kittens got larger, they started fighting. One day Babs and Baby had a big fight. And Babs, who was larger than Baby, won.

The Bible says that the lamb and the lion will lie down together in peace in heaven. Maybe there's an animal that you have seen at the zoo that you wish you could pet or even have as your own. But the animal must live in a cage because it might hurt you. In heaven there will be all kinds of animals, and the nice thing about it will be that the animals won't bite, and you will not have to be afraid of them. A little child shall lead them. —C.B.T.

Love Your Enemies

✳ *Love your enemies, do good to those who hate you, bless those who curse you, and pray for those who mistreat you. Luke 6:27, 28, TEV.*

Harry didn't want to cry. Crying only made Biff act worse, and he was already being really mean.

"You're the dumbest kid in the whole world," Biff said, riding alongside on his bike while Harry walked home from school. "It's a wonder you know enough to get out of bed in the morning."

Harry swallowed hard. He knew he wasn't dumb. Grandma said he was the smartest boy she'd ever seen.

"And that grandma you live with is the ugliest thing!"

Harry's hands made themselves into fists. Grandma took good care of him. She loved him.

"Yeah," Biff yelled, "you're about the dumbest—"

They'd reached Harry's walk, and he turned and went into the house as Grandma had said to do. Like she always did after school, she had milk and cookies waiting for him. He gave her a big hug.

"I'm glad to see you too," Grandma said. She looked at him. "Has that Biff boy been after you again?"

Harry nodded and told her what had happened.

"Well," Grandma said. "I'm glad you walked away, but it looks like we'll have to give that boy the treatment."

"The treatment?" Harry repeated in surprise. What did Grandma mean?

"You'll see," Grandma said. "Bow your head."

Harry bowed his head. "Dear Lord," Grandma said, "we pray for Biff. This boy's in trouble. Help us hold loving thoughts toward him and bless him, please. Amen."

Harry looked up. "But Grandma, why are we praying for Biff when he's so mean?"

Grandma grinned. "His meanness is the reason. A boy like that *needs* our prayers." She pushed the cookies toward Harry. "We've been really blessed by God, you know. We have each other to love."

Harry nodded. He bit into one of her gingerbread men. "Grandma," he said with a grin, "I think you're the smartest grandma in the world."

Grandma poured more milk into his glass. "We'll both be smart," she said, "as long as we listen to Jesus." —N.C.P.

A Happy Heart

A happy heart is like good medicine. Prov. 17:22, ICB.

O nce upon a time a young man got sick. He had a terrible disease, and the doctor told him that he wouldn't get well. "I'm sorry," the good doctor said, "but you'd better do everything you want to do right away, because you won't live very much longer."

The young man felt sad. He wanted to get well. He went to other doctors, who told him he couldn't get well. Finally he decided to see what the Bible said. He started reading. He found something in the Bible that made him hopeful. It said that being happy and laughing is like medicine.

The young man decided to try the Bible's advice. He watched the funniest programs he could find on TV. He asked his friends to find lots of funny jokes and all the good news they could. When they told him the jokes and good news, the man laughed and laughed. He watched funny movies and listened to jokes all the time. One day he discovered that he felt better. He didn't feel sad anymore. In fact, he was happy.

He went back to the doctor, who told him he was all better. The man went away rejoicing.

Have you ever noticed that you feel better when you're happy and having fun? and that you don't feel good at all when you're cross and upset? I've noticed that, so I try to be happy all the time. Why don't you do that too?—V.L.W.

The Elephant That Did More Than She Was Told

Jesus Christ is the same yesterday, today, and forever.
Heb. 13:8, TEV.

Alice was a circus elephant from India. She always did her jobs without being told. When the circus moved from place to place, she lifted the big animal cages onto the railroad cars. She helped the other elephants load the heavy wagons. Once the front wheels of a circus wagon rolled off a flatcar. Alice saw it hanging, ready to fall. Without being told, she quickly pushed it back onto the flatcar. Alice lived to be very old. For 110 years she was always the same, quick to obey and do more than she was told.

The circus always started with a big parade of animals. The elephants, covered with pretty blankets, marched at the front of the parade. Alice followed the band, walking behind the men who played the drums.

Somehow a little girl got away from her mother and daddy and began to run toward the elephants. Everyone feared that the elephants would step on her with their big feet. But Alice saw the little girl and hurried to her. With her long trunk she lifted the little girl. Then she walked over to where the people sat watching the parade. The mother reached out and called, "It's my baby." Alice laid the little girl in her mother's arms.

Then Alice walked back into the parade while the crowd of people cheered. Everyone clapped their hands because this kind, big elephant had saved the little girl's life. The circus trainer was not surprised, because he knew that Alice always saw what needed to be done and did it without being told.

Alice is something like Jesus, who is always the same today, yesterday, and tomorrow. You can be like Alice and Jesus too. When Mother asks you to help her pull weeds in the garden or set the table for lunch, do you always obey?

Let's be like Jesus and Alice, doing even more than we are told. — E.E.L.

A Good Friend

But there is a friend who sticks closer than a brother. Prov. 18:24, NIV.

Look out, Ben! That toolbox is falling!" Ted was shouting as he ran. He threw himself at Ben and knocked him out of the way, just barely in time. The toolbox missed them and fell to the ground a few inches away from where both little boys landed on the grass.

Some men were working on top of the school cafeteria when the big toolbox slipped and came flying down and hit the ground where Ben had been standing minutes before.

Ben and Ted were good friends, closer than brothers. They had known each other since they were 2 years old. They were 6 now, and nothing could separate them.

One of the other boys said, "Man, Ted, that heavy old toolbox could've fallen on you."

"Well," Ted said, "I didn't stop to think about that. I thought it was gonna hit Ben, so I had to get him out of the way."

Ted and Ben put their arms around each other's shoulders and walked toward the classroom, glad that they were OK.

We all have a special Friend, who sticks closer than a brother. Do you know who that friend is?—A.C.B.

Lost and Found

And I . . . will draw all peoples to Myself. John 12:32, NKJV.

O h, no!" Brenda shouted. "We've left the key inside! Now what do we do?"

"I don't know," said Karen, "but Judy sure will be mad if we lose her key."

Brenda and Karen had gone swimming at the beach. Usually they took good care of Judy's key to the bathhouse. But this day, just as they were going out the door, the lock snapped shut. The girls had left the key inside on the bench.

Then Karen remembered that she had a small magnet at home. She raced home and soon returned with the magnet attached to a long string. Bravely Karen climbed up to the top of the building, which was covered with chicken wire. She tried to look down inside, but it was pitch dark down there—she couldn't see a thing!

Fishing for the lost key, she let the magnet down through one of the round openings, but nothing happened. She pulled it up, and then let it down a second time through another round opening. This time she heard "click!" and pulled up the key to safety.

In many ways we are like that little lost key. And by a cord of love Jesus was let down to us on this earth, where all is dark. His love is like a magnet, drawing us close to Him. Will you allow Jesus' love to draw you to Him today and every day?—P.H.

Jesus Helps Us

So, trust the Lord always. Isa. 26:4, ICB.

Richard Coffen is a book editor at the Review and Herald Publishing Association in Hagerstown, Maryland. The Christmas he was 6 years old, something happened that helped him learn to trust Jesus.

"This is great, Daddy!" Richard turned his round face upward to give Daddy one of his brightest smiles. Daddy patted Richard's light-brown hair and then turned to fasten a white sheet to the living room wall.

"My very own movie projector!" Richard said to himself and to everyone else in the room. He scooted onto the sofa and settled back to watch the *Our Gang* cartoon.

"Lights out, please!" Daddy called to Mother as he flipped the switch on the movie projector. But there was no picture.

"I'll check to make sure the plug is in properly," Daddy said, scrambling to the wall socket. The plug was in. So Daddy flipped the switch again. No picture. Daddy flipped the switch off and then back on. He jiggled the projector. He flipped and jiggled, flipped and jiggled. "Lights on, Mother," he finally said sadly.

"I guess we'd better ask Jesus to fix this projector, Daddy," Richard said. And Richard started praying right away: "Dear Jesus, please make my projector work. It's my Christmas present. Amen. Lights out, please, Mother!"

Daddy flipped the switch. And just as the *Our Gang* cartoon appeared on the sheet, Richard said, "I guess we'd better turn off the projector and thank Jesus." This time Richard knelt beside the projector. "Thank You, Jesus," he prayed.

Richard watched the *Our Gang* cartoon at least twice that day. And he used that projector to watch many, many other movies while he was a little boy. Each time he flipped the switch, he remembered that Jesus had fixed his projector.

Why do you think Jesus fixed the projector?

What special thing has Jesus done for you?—F.J.C.

Peach Ice Cream

✺ *Children, obey your parents in the Lord, for this is right.*
Eph. 6:1, NKJV.

Crystal lay down on the soft grass and looked up at the clouds in the sky. She had helped Mother weed the garden and wash the lunch dishes. Now she was tired and wanted to rest in the backyard. The white fluffy clouds above her formed many sizes and shapes. Some of them looked like animals. She had just spotted a cloud that looked like a snowman when Mother called her name. Crystal lay very still and pretended to be asleep.

"Crystal, please come here," Mother called again.

Crystal didn't answer. Finally Mother went back inside the house. Crystal chased a butterfly around the flower bed and then went into the kitchen to get a drink of water.

There sat Mother and Daddy at the kitchen table. They were finishing a bowl of peach ice cream.

"Where's mine?" Crystal asked.

"There's not any more," Daddy explained. "The freezer broke, and the ice cream was melting. We had to eat it before it melted."

"Why didn't you call me?" Crystal asked. "I want some ice cream too."

"I *did* call you," Mother answered. "But you chose not to come when I called. I thought you didn't want to be bothered."

Crystal decided right then always to obey when Mother called. She knew that Mother loved her.

Do you think we should always obey Jesus? What kind of good gifts does Jesus give you?—C.B.E.

You Don't Have to Like It

☀ *[God] gives food to every living creature. Ps. 136:25, ICB.*

Priska had not yet eaten her breakfast. She sat staring at her bowl of oatmeal and whined, "Do I *have* to eat it?"

"Yes," said Mother.

"But I don't like it."

"You don't have to like it. Remember, we choose some food like oats, rice, barley, cream of wheat, not just because we like them, but because they are good for us," Mother said.

Jamie skipped into the house, washed his hands, and hurried to the dinner table. "Salad *again*? Do I have to eat it?"

"Yes, Jamie," said Mother.

"But I don't like it."

"Your salad has tomatoes, cucumbers, and lettuce in it. God made good vegetables because He knew they would be good for our bodies. We eat them not just because we like them, but because they're good for us."

George had a little bowl of peaches for dessert, but he really wanted a cookie instead. "Do I have to eat it?"

"Yes," said Mother.

"But I don't like peaches."

"I know, but you don't have to like them. God made good fruit because He knows what's best for our bodies."

We eat the good food that God made because we know it is good for us. God knows best. When you to go to bed at night, do you like it? No. But you go because you know we have to get sleep so that we can grow strong and healthy. So when you sit down to eat and find something you don't like on your plate say, "I don't like it, but I'll eat it because I know it's good for me."—E.G.N.

The Poor

If you make fun of poor people, you insult the God who made them. Prov. 17:5, TEV.

Jenny watched Grandma frost the cake—round and round the icing swirled. Grandma looked up and smiled. "You're looking serious today," she said. "Don't tell me you don't like chocolate frosting anymore."

Jenny grinned. "Of course I like it. It's my favorite."

"Then why the big frown?"

"It's the new girl," Jenny said. "She wears the funniest clothes."

Grandma put some leftover frosting on a spoon and gave it to Jenny. "What do you mean, funny?"

Jenny licked the frosting. "Ummm! Grandma, this is good." Jenny thought about Carol for a minute. "Well, her clothes look awfully old. And they're too small."

Grandma said, "Go on, tell me the rest."

Jenny smiled. Grandma always knew when there was more. "Well, some of the boys were making fun of her, calling her names."

Grandma started looking concerned. "That's not good."

Jenny nodded. "Carol looked like she was going to cry. Grandma, why were those boys mean to her?"

Grandma shook her head. "I don't know, Jenny. Sometimes people are mean to each other. But I know one thing—God's doesn't like it when we behave that way."

"Why not?" Jenny asked. She knew Grandma could tell her.

Grandma put another swirl on the cake. "It says right in the Bible that people who make fun of the poor are insulting the God who made them. Poor people belong to God too."

Jenny finished licking the frosting off the spoon. "This is your best frosting ever," she said. She looked at the cake. Then she looked at Grandma. "Maybe I can ask Carol to come over after school tomorrow and have a piece of cake."

Grandma smiled. "That's a great idea. I'd like to meet her."—N.C.P.

Always Room for You

✻ *Give thanks to the Lord, for his love endures for ever.* Ps. 107:1, REB.

Grandpa sold his big old house and moved into a small apartment. Ian worried. "Now I can't come to stay with you, because there won't be room for me."

Grandpa said, "There's a spare bedroom in my apartment. You can stay there when you come to visit."

"Whew!" Ian said.

Grandpa laughed. "Ian, no matter where I live, there will always be room for you."

"But what if you move to a *smaller* apartment and there's only one bedroom—for you?" Ian asked.

"Then," Grandpa said, "you'd sleep on one side of the bed, and I'd sleep on the other."

"But what if you moved to just a room and you got a tiny cot? There wouldn't be room for me then."

"Of course there would!" Grandpa said. "You could sleep on the old recliner chair."

"And what if you had to move out, Grandpa, and you were a homeless person?"

"I doubt my family would let that happen . . ." Grandpa began.

"But what if it *did* happen, Grandpa?"

Grandpa sighed. "Then I'd find a shopping cart, and I'd push you around in it. See? There'd still be room for you."

"What if the shopping cart broke, Grandpa, and you didn't have it anymore?"

Grandpa's eyes twinkled. "There would still be room for you."

"Where, Grandpa? Where?"

"Right here," Grandpa said, holding out his arms.

Ian ran into them and snuggled against the warmest, coziest, roomiest place of all.

"Any more questions?" Grandpa asked.

"No, Grandpa," Ian said. "I know there's always room for me!"— V.L.K.

A Good-Bad Plan

✳ *Plans succeed when you get advice from many others.* Prov. 15:22, ICB.

Digging this well is harder than hauling buckets of water to the cucumber garden," Randy complained after many hours of digging. He pushed his glasses back up on his sweaty nose. "Another hour of digging will save us a lot of walking up and down Daniel Boone Trail, though," he said.

"Well, stop standing around and get busy!" David said with a grin. Randy wrinkled his nose at his brother and pushed his cowboy hat down over his strawberry-blond hair.

The brothers and their two buddies shoveled fast for another hour. "Water!" the boys shouted, scrambling out of the hole as it filled with muddy water.

"Yahoo!" Randy sung out, throwing his cowboy hat into the air. "Let's water some cucumbers!"

The boys scooped up buckets of muddy water and lugged them to the garden. A half hour had passed before the watering was done. "Humph!" Randy muttered, stopping to take a closer look at a cucumber plant. Quickly standing up, Randy called to David, "I think we've got a . . . a . . ."

"A problem!" his father's voice boomed above his head. "What happened here?"

Talking all at once, and pointing, and dragging Mr. Fishell by his arms, the boys led him to their well.

"It's a fine well!" Mr. Fishell praised the boys. "But I'm afraid that the muddy water will kill the plants."

"Oh, no!" the boys moaned.

"Come on, now. I'll help you wash the mud off the plants," Mr. Fishell said.

After the cucumber plants were all cleaned, the sad-faced boys sat on the wet ground.

"Today things did not work out the way you wanted them to, boys," Mr. Fishell said. "But haven't you learned something?"

"Yes!" they quickly answered.

"You can never have too much help!"

"Tell a grown-up about your great new ideas . . ."

". . . *before* you do a lot of hard work . . ."

". . . and before you get covered with mud!"

Whom do you share your ideas with?

[Note to parents: Randy Fishell is associate editor of *Guide* magazine.]—F.J.C.

Daring Denny

☀ *Children, obey your parents in all things. This pleases the Lord.*
Col. 3:20, ICB.

Two-year-old Denny stomped a tiny foot into the eaves trough along the edge of the porch roof. It wiggled and scrunched a little, because it was very old. And it was made to catch the rain—not for little boys to walk in!

Mother called frantically from the bedroom window, "Denny! Come back!"

"No," replied Denny, as he took another daring step in the eaves trough. "I fly, Mommy! I fly!" he exclaimed.

"No, no! Denny, come here quickly!" Mommy tried to climb out the window that Denny had crawled through to get on the roof, but she didn't fit very well! Denny laughed and ran to the far corner of the roof. He thought that she was playing a game with him and that he was winning!

"Me birdie!" he called to Mommy, and he bent his legs to leap into the air.

"Stop! *Stop!*" Mother ordered.

That was even more fun for Denny. Laughing, he raced back and forth on the roof.

Mother prayed that Jesus would keep Denny safe. Then she opened her arms wide and said, "Denny, come give Mommy a big hug."

"No," said Denny, now stomping with both feet in the shaky rain catcher.

Mom had another idea. "Come play with your fire truck, Denny."

Denny didn't talk much yet, but he understood fire truck. Fire truck was fun, too. Suddenly he ran to Mother's open arms. She pulled him inside and hugged him so tightly he struggled to get away.

"Play truck," he pleaded.

"OK," said Mom. "But first you will have to sit in the time-out chair and think. You must learn to obey." She sat him in the little chair in the corner. "Jesus gives children mommies and daddies to help keep them from being hurt and to help them grow up strong and happy. If you had fallen off the porch roof, you would have been hurt very badly. And you might have been killed—like the little bird that fell out of its nest onto the sidewalk yesterday."

Tears came into Denny's big blue eyes as he remembered bringing Mommy the little birdie that couldn't move, couldn't eat, and couldn't sing or fly.

His time-out must have seemed very long, but finally he said, "Mommy, I not fly. I play truck!"

Mommy hugged him, and together they thanked Jesus for keeping Denny safe even when he disobeyed.

"WOO-oooo-OOOOOooooo-ooo!" said the fire truck. "Whoo-OOO-ooo," said Denny. —B.V.

Sisters Are Gifts

☀ *Every perfect gift is from God. James 1:17, ICB.*

If the baby is a *girl*, we're keeping her!" Norma wagged a finger at her school teacher to make sure she understood. "We have too many boys already." Norma thought for a second about the latest trick her brothers had played on her. "But if the baby is a *boy*, you can pick up the furniture and him the same day he comes home from the hospital," Norma said in her most grown-up voice.

With that business taken care of, Norma dashed to the yellow school bus. She could hardly wait to get back home from school so that she could check on Mother. "I'm home, Mother!" Norma called out while rushing toward the kitchen, where Mother was making soup.

As soon as Mother turned away from the stove, Norma placed her hand on Mother's tummy. "I can feel her kicking!" Norma squealed. "Tomorrow is Christmas Eve. Do you think my sister will be born before Christmas, Mother?"

Mother laid the soupspoon on the table and took Norma's hands in hers. "I'm sure the baby is going to be born very soon, Norma," Mother said. "But we can't be sure that the baby is a girl."

"I'm sure enough for everybody!" Norma said. But before she climbed into bed that night, Norma prayed again, "Dear Jesus, please be sure to send me a little sister. Thank You. Amen."

On the morning of Christmas Eve Norma awakened to hear her noisy brothers yelling, "Daddy took Mother to the hospital! Mother's gone to the hospital, Norma!"

Norma just couldn't sit still. She rushed around the house, stopping every few minutes to peek into the room Mother had prepared for the baby.

Ring! Ring! Ring!

"Daddy!" Norma hollered. She raced to get close to the phone before her brothers could crowd her out.

"Her name is Carol," Grandma said as soon as she hung up the phone.

"My Christmas Carol!" Norma whooped as she hopped around the room! "Christmas is especially wonderful because of Carol!"

185

Tiny Carol became very sick and had to stay in the hospital several days longer than usual. But finally Norma and her brothers got a chance to see Carol and to kiss her little cheek. "She's a gift from God!" Norma told her brothers. And for once they didn't call Norma a silly girl.

Do you think that sisters and brothers are gifts from God? How can we act so that everyone will know that we're gifts from God?

[Note to parents: Pastor Norma Sahlin is director of advancement for Takoma Academy in Takoma Park, Maryland.]—F.J.C.

The Bird That Lived

❋ Jesus said to her, "I am the resurrection and the life; he who believes in me, though he die, yet shall he live." John 11:25, RSV.

One day at church in Singapore I saw a pretty bird fly through the open door. First it hit the wall. Then it saw a green plant and started for it. But on the way the bird flew into a row of chairs. When I picked it up, the little bird lay limp in my hand. I was afraid that it had a broken neck.

How did this blue, green, red, and yellow bird ever get into the big city? I wondered. Its home was in the jungle. As it lay in my lap, I could feel its heartbeat, so I knew that the bird wasn't dead. For 15 minutes the tiny body did not move. Then I saw the bird open one eye and move a leg. Then it was still again. Was the bird dying? More time passed. The bird moved again. Maybe it would live.

I slipped out the door and found some water. I opened the bird's beak and let several drops fall from my finger into its mouth. The bird swallowed. More drops. Slowly its eyes opened as the bird drank more water. Then it gave a little squawk! It tried to get away. I knew now that the neck wasn't broken and that soon the bird would fly.

Across the street was a park. I took the bird there. Before I got to the trees, it began trying to get free. How happy I felt as I opened my hand and watched the bird fly away!

I thought of the day when Jesus will come back and wake up the people who have died. When they hear Jesus call, "Wake up!" they will be like that pretty bird. The dead people will rise up to meet Jesus in the air. Maybe your grandma or grandpa or someone else you love has died. If that person loved Jesus, he or she will wake up and live with Him forever. —E.E.L.

Forgotten!

☀ *Can a mother forget her little child? . . . Yet even if that should be, I will not forget you. Isa. 49:15, TLB.*

Summer school for Dad was over. The apartment was empty, and the car packed. Five-year-old Carol checked all the closets to make sure nothing was left behind.

"Let's go," called Dad.

"I'll be right there, but let me walk over and tell Mrs. Barton goodbye," Mother called.

"I'll pick you up at her apartment," Dad answered as he grabbed the car keys. Mrs. Barton lived around the corner a half block away in another apartment building.

A little later Carol came out of the bedroom. Where was everyone? Mom, Dad, and younger sister Laura had disappeared. Carol had not heard Dad call. Carol ran outside and looked down over the railing. The car was gone! Carol had been left.

Crying softly, she walked over to the outside stairs and sat down. Children playing in the area came to comfort her.

After a few minutes Mom came to the car where Dad and Laura were waiting. She was surprised that Carol was not with Dad. Of course, Dad was surprised that Carol was not with Mom. Quickly they drove back to their apartment building.

Seeing teary-eyed Carol, Dad jumped from the car, ran over to the group of children, and hugged Carol. Carol had not been forgotten for long!

Even if a mom and dad might forget their child, our text today tells us that God will never forget us! Aren't you glad! —P.M.M.

So Hard to Choose

✳ *Choose for yourselves this day whom you will serve.* Joshua 24:15, NIV.

O ne year instead of buying and wrapping a special birthday present for Jill, her grandmother did something different. She took the little girl to a big store that had shelves and shelves of stuffed animals. "Jill," Grandma said, "I want you to choose any animal here. Take as much time as you need, and be sure it's the one you really want. Then I'll buy it for you, and it will be yours for a long, long time."

Jill's eyes opened wide. "Any animal, Grandma?"

"Any animal," Grandma said again.

So Jill looked at stuffed bears and rabbits. She looked at stuffed cats and dogs and lions; giraffes and monkeys and frogs; dinosaurs and every kind of animal. "It's so hard to choose," she said, and kept on looking.

A long time later she picked up a beautiful stuffed raccoon with a mask across its eyes that made it look like a bandit. It had stripes on its tail. "I like this one best of all."

So did Grandma. She paid for the raccoon and took Jill home.

Know what? Jill kept her raccoon all the way through grade school and high school. She just graduated from college, and she still has the beautiful little stuffed animal! She also remembers the special day when Grandma got it for her.

We have to make many choices in our lives. The most important choice is to choose to follow Jesus and to invite Him to live in our hearts to be our friend and Saviour. If you haven't done this, now is the best time of all. He loves you and wants you to love Him so that He can guide and care for you. —C.L.R.

Love Jesus

If you love me, you will obey my commandments. John 14:15, TEV.

Vicki frowned. Why did Daddy have to stop to help Mrs. Peterson with her groceries? This was the day he had promised to go to the park for their special bike ride.

Vicki bit her bottom lip. It seemed like they never got to do what they started out to do, because Daddy was always stopping to help people.

Finally Mrs. Peterson and her groceries were all inside her house. Daddy came back, whistling cheerfully. He looked at Vicki. "Why such a gloomy face?"

"You promised to ride bikes," Vicki said, "but you stopped to help Mrs. Peterson instead."

"Yes, I stopped to help her," Daddy said, "but why should that give you a face like sour apples?"

Vicki tried to explain: "You were supposed to ride with me."

Daddy got on his bike. "I *am* riding with you."

He pedaled off toward the park, and Vicki rode beside him.

"Jesus told us to help each other," Daddy said. "That's why I stopped at Mrs. Peterson's. She hasn't any children to help her."

Vicki thought about that. "But you're always helping people," she said.

Daddy nodded. "People who love Jesus obey His commandments. And He told us that we should help each other."

Vicki thought of all the things Daddy did to help people. Lots and lots of things. Then she grinned. "After we finish our ride, maybe we can stop back to see if we can help Mrs. Peterson with something else. And this time I won't look like sour apples. This time I'll help too."

"Great!" Daddy said. "That's my girl. Race you to that pine tree!"—N.C.P.

The Welcoming

As I have loved you, so you must love one another. John 13:34, NIV.

Nobody sat beside Lisa in her new kindergarten Sabbath school room. No one even looked at her, and she felt strange. The other girls and boys all knew each other. They laughed and played together before Sabbath school began. Lisa didn't want to be there. She wanted Mommy.

A big tear rolled down her cheek. Another followed it.

Then Lisa saw a little dark-haired girl looking at her. The little girl smiled. Then she waved. Lisa didn't smile back. Her hand didn't wave either. She blinked her eyes and wiped a tear away.

When she took her hand down, the little girl with dark hair sat in the chair beside her. "Hi! I'm Kristy. Would you like to come and sit beside me? Or should I sit here?"

Lisa swallowed and cleared her throat. "I'll come with you," she finally said. Kristy helped her with all the songs and flannels and everything. When Lisa dropped a stuffed animal, Kristy laughed and handed it back to her.

Lisa had fun! She felt happy that she'd come.

Could you be a friend to someone new in your Sabbath school? Did you know that would make Jesus happy? It would make the new person happy too. And it would even make you happy. Do it!—V.L.W.

Miracle

Not even one of the little birds can die without your Father's knowing it. Matt. 10:29, ICB.

Davy held the tiny little animal in his hands. "Mom, Mom, look at the little animal," whispered Davy. "I found it under the cherry tree."

"It looks like a baby squirrel, Davy. It's so brand new that its eyes are still sealed shut," Mother said. "It has two bite marks on its side and one on its stomach. It looks like you rescued this baby from a cat."

"I went to swing on the rope and almost stepped on this tiny animal," said Davy. "It is so thin that I can see the heart beating. How can we help this squirrel get better?"

"Why don't you give me the baby while you collect a shoe box, a heating pad, and an old towel," Mother said.

Davy rushed off to get a shoe box from under the bed. He slipped to his knees and whispered a prayer to Jesus. "You helped me not to step on the baby squirrel. Please help us take care of it."

Mother plugged in the heating pad. They placed it in the bottom of the shoe box and made a nest out of the old towel.

"I found this bottle in the cupboard under the sink," Davy said. "What can we give the squirrel to eat?"

"If I remember right, we can use the puppy formula," Mother said.

Mother helped Davy fix puppy formula. Davy held the baby squirrel and set its long squarish head on his thumb. Mother gently slipped the nipple of the bottle into the squirrel's mouth. She wiggled the bottle up and down so that a drop came out. "It doesn't know how to eat," Davy sighed.

Mother smiled. "Poor little thing has been so cold and frightened, it will have to get used to us. Let's fix these sore spots."

Davy helped Mother put medicine on the spots. He was afraid he'd hurt the little animal.

Davy helped Mother feed the squirrel every two hours until bedtime. Then they put the box by his bed. Mother explained, "I'll come in during the night to feed the squirrel. It has to eat often to keep from getting hungry."

In the morning when Daddy told him it was time to get up, Davy wasn't sure if he should look in the box. He decided to talk to Jesus first. "Please help me to be brave enough to see if the baby squirrel is all right."

Just then he heard a little scratching noise. He lifted the lid of the box and found the baby squirrel in the corner.

"Look, Mom, the squirrel is hungry," Davy called as he carried the squirrel down the stairs. "May I feed it?"

Mother had a bottle ready. Davy carefully fed the squirrel. "The baby really is stronger today!" Davy said as he laughed. "I'd like to name the squirrel Miracle. I'm sure Jesus helped me see this baby before I stepped on it, and He helped the little squirrel learn to eat so it can get stronger." —L.R.

Too Many Dolls

Love is . . . never . . . selfish or rude. 1 Cor. 13:4, 5, TLB.

Gillian and Maria loved playing dolls together. Gillian's doll was Lindsay. Maria's doll was Chelsea.

One day Aunt Cheryl came and brought them a beautiful new doll to share.

First they argued terribly over what to name her. "Enough!" Mom yelled. "I'm naming her Mimi."

The sisters could never decide whose turn it was to play with Mimi. They screamed and fought.

Mom separated them, and all would be quiet for a while, until they were together again with all three dolls.

One afternoon both girls reached for Mimi and tugged at her until her clothing ripped. "Look what you did!" they shouted at each other. Mom sent them to separate rooms.

When everyone was calmer, Mom called them together. "You have too many dolls," she declared.

"Too many dolls?" Gillian gasped. "We have only three. Our friend Eve has 20 all her own!"

"You have too many dolls," Mom repeated. "Anything that makes you act unloving isn't worth having. Unless you learn to share, Mimi will have to go."

The girls thought about their problem. Finally Gillian said, "You know how Mom and Dad share doing the dishes every other day? That's what we can do!"

"Good idea," agreed Maria.

Gillian said, "I get Mimi on Mondays, Wednesdays, and Fridays. You get her on Sundays, Tuesdays, and Thursdays."

"And she can rest on Sabbaths," Maria said. "That way she won't get into any trouble."

(And she didn't!) — V.L.K.

Grown-up Friends

✷ Listen to instruction and grow wise. Prov. 8:33, NEB.

Hey, Stevie Boy!" Mr. Washington called down the street to Stephen Ruff. *Stevie always looks neat in those blue pants and that green plaid shirt*, Mr. Washington said to himself.

"Hey, Mr. Washington!" Stevie called back as he turned onto the sidewalk leading to the green house.

Mr. Washington disappeared into the house and quickly returned, carrying two large slices of juicy watermelon.

"Thank you," Stevie said. He plopped down on the grass near the porch step. Mr. Washington settled into an old chair on the porch. The two friends took turns spitting little brown watermelon seeds into a bushel basket. For a while the only sounds were the *plip! plip!* of seeds against the wood and Stevie's belly laughs whenever he "made a basket."

"You're a great seed spitter, Mr. Washington!" Stevie said.

"One of the best!" Mr. Washington agreed.

Suddenly one of Stevie's seeds landed in Mr. Washington's black-and-white hair. This time Stevie doubled over with laughter.

"You're a champion laugher," Mr. Washington said.

"One of the best!" Stevie agreed.

From beneath his bushy eyebrows Mr. Washington's reddened eyes smiled at Stevie.

Soon the watermelon rind was bare, and as usual, Mr. Washington began to talk about more important things. Stevie listened carefully.

"How are you doing in school, Stevie Boy?" Mr. Washington began. "Stay in school, Stevie. Stay away from troublemakers. You have a chance to make a better life than I have."

Stevie's elderly friend asked more questions and told him a lot of helpful hints about how to behave and what to say.

"Yes, Mr. Washington," and "I'll try, Mr. Washington," Stevie would answer. And Stevie did stay in school and out of trouble. Today he is the editor of *Message* magazine, a magazine that is sent around the world to tell people about Jesus.

Do you listen carefully when grown-ups tell you how to stay happy and safe?

Let's thank Jesus for giving us wise grown-ups for friends. —F.J.C.

Ouch!

✵ *Children, obey your parents in the Lord: for this is right.* Eph. 6:1.

A nn's family lived on the second floor of a three-story house. She liked the house. Especially the banister that ran along the stairs in the front hallway. It was like having her own private sliding board. Sliding down the banister was a lot of fun! It beat walking down all those stairs! Ann could easily slide down the banister and be at the bottom in record time.

But Ann's parents had said, "No sliding down the bannister." What would make them say such a thing? Boy, parents could sure take the fun out of fun things sometimes!

One day Ann had gone outside to play with her brothers. They were having a good time playing kickball, but when she asked if she could play with them, they quickly told her no. There was nothing exciting or fun for her to do. Ann didn't want to ride her scooter, and the wagon needed another person for pulling or pushing.

What fun thing could she do by herself? Ann sat down on the step with her hand in her chin. *There's nothing for me to do*, she said to herself. She thought for a moment and then remembered the banister in the front hallway of her house.

She ran around to the front of the house and went inside to the hallway. Looking up the stairs to the beginning of the banister, she could just see herself sliding all the way down. Slowly Ann began climbing the stairs. It seemed that with each step she took, she could hear a little voice saying, *No sliding down the banister! No sliding down the banister!*

Reaching the top of the stairs, Ann put her hands on the banister, climbed on, and started her slide down to the bottom. What fun! How fast she could go! Suddenly, though, Ann yelled in pain, "Ouch! Ouch! Mommy! Mommy!"

Mother came quickly and found Ann sitting halfway down the banister. Tears were running down her cheeks. "What is it, Ann? What's the matter?" asked Mother.

197

"Mommy, something is hurting my leg. Ouch! It hurts bad," cried Ann.

Ann's daddy came out to see what the crying was about. He lifted Ann off the banister and carried her up the stairs into her little bedroom. Then Daddy looked at Ann's leg. There deep in her skin was a long splinter from the rough wood of the banister. Oh, how it hurt while Daddy took that splinter out!

When Ann was tempted to do something that Mommy or Daddy had told her not to do, she remembered the splinter from the banister, and she obeyed.

Jesus is happy when we obey. —C.B.T.

Ducks Can Love Too

The greatest love a person can have for his friends is to give his life for them. John 15:13, TEV.

Susie had a pet duck named Waddles. When she played in the sandbox, Waddles stayed beside her. When she chased butterflies in the yard, Waddles followed her. Whenever Susie was outside, Waddles was right with her.

When Susie got a new baby sister, Carol, Waddles loved her too. Sometimes Mother put the baby outside in the buggy. Waddles always sat beneath the buggy and watched so that nothing would hurt the baby. Mother liked to have Waddles care for baby Carol, because sometimes Susie and her friends would forget to shut the back gate. Anything that entered the backyard would leave fast when Waddles used his sharp beak to chase it away.

One morning when Waddles sat underneath the baby buggy in the yard, Mother got a phone call from a neighbor. "I just saw a fierce-looking dog in your driveway."

Could Susie have left the gate open? Mother wondered. As she rushed outside, she heard a loud "Quack, quack!" from Waddles. The big dog was just a few feet from the baby. The duck had begun to fight the dog. Mother grabbed the baby and ran into the house.

Quickly she called the police for help. She could hear the terrible fight going on in the backyard—growls, barks, loud quacks, and flapping wings. If only Waddles would fly away from the danger! But no, the brave duck would not allow the dog near the buggy, even though Mother had taken the baby into the house. When the police arrived, Waddles' bloody body covered the entrance to the backyard. He had given his life for his little friend.

Waddles reminds us of Jesus. Jesus fought the enemy, Satan, for you. Jesus died because He loves each boy and girl. He gladly gave His live to save you, so that you, His little friends, can live in heaven with Him. —E.E.L.

Steven Puts It Off

Behold, I am coming soon! Rev. 22:12, NIV.

Steven had been going to Vacation Bible School every night. His teacher had been telling him that Jesus loved him very much and wanted Steven to love Him too.

Night after night Steven learned more and more about Jesus. He learned that Jesus was preparing a special place in heaven for him and is coming back to take him to that place. Steven was happy about all he was learning. He wanted to ask Jesus to come into his heart. He wanted to live for Jesus and go to heaven with Him when He comes.

Each night Steven thought, *I'll do it tonight.* But he kept putting it off. Finally there was just one more night left for Vacation Bible School. Would Steven give his life to Jesus that night? No. Steven put it off again. He returned home that night and went to sleep. His sleep was interrupted by a scream. It was his scream. Steven woke up crying and screaming.

His mother rushed into his room. "Steven, are you all right? What's the matter, honey?"

Between sobs Steven sniffed out his dream. "Mommy, . . . sniff, sniff, . . . I dreamed that Jesus . . . sniff . . . that Jesus came and that I wasn't ready to see Him."

"Why, honey?"

"Mommy, I've been putting off giving my heart to Jesus. I want to do it right now." Steven prayed, "Dear Jesus, I'm sorry I've been putting off giving my life to You. Come into my heart, Lord Jesus. I want to go home with You when You come. Thank You, Jesus. I love You. Amen."

Jesus said that He will come again for those who love Him. Have you asked Jesus to come into your heart? If not, you can do that right now. If you have, thank Jesus for being with you all the time. — E.G.N.

Led by an Angel

For there stood by me this night an angel. Acts 27:23, NKJV.

Mommy, Daddy, Candice, and Brandon were building their dream house in the country. Slowly but surely the house began to go up. The men worked and worked and sawed and hammered for a long, long time.

Then one day, as they were getting ready to move into their new house, Daddy got a call to move to another state and work at a job that would help people learn about Jesus. Mommy fasted and prayed for three whole days, because she wanted to know God's will.

Mommy prayed and prayed. By the second day there was still no answer. But that evening, as she was putting away some groceries, 5-year-old Candice looked up and said, "Mommy, we're going to move to Illinois."

"How do you know that, honey?" Mommy asked.

"Because last night, when I was sleeping, an angel stood next to my bed and told me that we are going to take all our food, clothes, and toys, and move to Illinois. The angel had on a white robe and had wings," she said with excitement. "It was very bright, and the angel was *this* tall, Mommy!" Candice pointed up to the ceiling.

A tear began to roll down Mommy's cheek. She knew that God had answered her prayer in a wonderful way. She was very happy. But she was also a little sad because she realized that they would never live in the house they had worked so hard to build. Then Mommy remembered that in heaven there is a beautiful mansion waiting for all those who are faithful. That one will be better than any house we can build on earth. Don't you think so?—P.H.

Balancing Act

☀ *Children, obey your parents in all things. This pleases the Lord.*
Col. 3:20, ICB.

Marjorie, I want you to take these old paint cans to the trash bin," called Mother as she was getting ready for Sabbath. "Be very careful because some of them still have paint in them."

"I'll be right there, Mother," replied Marjorie. She quickly set down her doll and ran to help Mother.

Daddy had used the cans of paint to trim his big yellow tow truck. He had used yellow, green, black, and orange paint for the job. Oh, how pretty that old truck had looked when he had finished!

Marjorie looked at the cans stacked in the corner. There were so many cans that it would take her several trips to get them all to the trash bin by the road. Marjorie was eager to get back to playing with her dolls. How could she get the job done quickly? Suddenly Marjorie got a bright idea. Why not do a balancing act? It would be lots of fun to pile the cans on her head and take them out to the trash bin all at once. Then she could get back to her dolls.

The yellow can was the largest, so she placed it on her head first. Next came green, then black and yellow, and last of all the orange. Marjorie walked very carefully toward the back door. This was fun! But it was slow going. *When I get outside, I'll be able to walk faster*, she told herself.

Marjorie hadn't noticed the small red car that her little brother had left on the doorstep right outside the back door. Her foot slipped on the car, and she lost her balance. Down she went, paint cans and all, in a big heap on the ground.

"Oh, Mother! Help! Help!" cried Marjorie, sitting on the ground with paint buckets all around her. Mother came running from the living room. She gasped! Marjorie looked more like a modern art painting rather than her pretty little girl. Some of the lids had come off the paint cans when Marjorie fell, and the beautiful colors were dripping through her hair, off her nose, and all over her nice clean dress. From Mother's expression, Marjorie knew that Mother didn't know whether to laugh or to cry.

"Well, Marjorie," Mother said at last, "there's only one way to clean up this mess. Come into the backyard, and I'll get the turpentine."

The turpentine did a good job of removing the paint, but the scrubbing did something else to Marjorie's tender skin. When Mother got through with her, she looked like a big red tomato! Oh, how her skin stung from that turpentine!

You can be sure Marjorie remembered for a long time that when Mother said "Be careful" there was a good reason. —M.K.S.

The Key

✳ [Jesus] is the key that opens all the hidden treasures of God's wisdom and knowledge. Col. 2:3, TEV.

Jeff watched Grandpa pound a nail into the birdhouse. "I wish I knew how to do that," Jeff said.

Grandpa smiled. "You will one day."

Jeff shook his head. One day was too far away. "I don't know if I can ever learn it all."

Grandpa chuckled. "Nobody can learn it all, boy." He pounded in another nail, so neatly that Jeff could hardly see it.

"I guess not," Jeff said. "But learning even part of it is hard work."

Grandpa nodded. "There's a lot more to learn today than when I was a boy, but you can do it."

Jeff frowned. "Our teacher said learning is like hunting for buried treasure."

Grandpa nodded. "She's right. But there's one treasure you've already got."

Jeff thought hard. Treasure meant chests and gold, lots of money. His piggy bank was almost empty. "Grandpa, are you sure? I don't think I have any treasure."

Grandpa screwed a hook into the top of the birdhouse. "Sure, you do," he said. "It tells you right in the Bible how to get to God's treasures of wisdom and knowledge."

Jeff thought really hard, so hard that his face scrunched up into a frown, but he still didn't know what Grandpa meant.

"The Bible tells us about a key," Grandpa said, holding the finished birdhouse up for Jeff to see.

"A key?" Jeff said. "But the Bible's not about keys, it's about—"

Jeff saw the twinkle in Grandpa's eyes. Grandpa grinned at him. "Say it, boy. Say it."

"The Bible's about Jesus!" Jeff said.

"Right," Grandpa agreed. "And Jesus is the key to everything." He put the birdhouse down and gave Jeff a big hug. —N.C.P.

The Gift

✺ *I am with you always. Matt. 28:20, NIV.*

Ebony was thinking about riding in the elevator, the little room that carries people up and down in her apartment building. This is how she travels from the thirteenth floor, where she lives, to the main floor. Ebony must ride the elevator when she wants to go to Grandmother's house, and that is where she will celebrate being 5 years old today.

"But Mama, when the elevator moves downward, my stomach feels jumpy!" Ebony said, her brown eyes filling with big tears. "And my ears hurt, too!" Ebony stomped her foot so hard that the blue ribbons on her short, thick braids bounced up and down.

Just then someone knocked at their door.

"Grandma!" Ebony shouted when Mama opened the door.

"I wanted to give you my gift before the party," Grandma said, and handed her a little pink box.

"My own little tape recorder!" Ebony shouted after opening the gift.

As soon as she pushed the shiny "Play" button, Ebony heard Grandma singing: " 'Anywhere with Jesus I can safely go, anywhere He leads me in this world below.' "

Mama and Daddy started singing along. Ebony joined in on the chorus. Then Grandma whispered in Ebony's ear, "Jesus always rides in the elevator with us."

Grandma held Ebony's hand as they walked toward the elevator. Before the elevator doors closed, the neighbors could hear Ebony singing loudly, " 'Anywhere with Jesus I can safely go!' "

Is there some place where you feel afraid? The park? In bed when all the lights are out? In Sabbath school without Mama or Daddy? Remember that wherever you are, Jesus is there to keep you safe.

["Anywhere With Jesus" is Number 508 of *The Seventh-day Adventist Hymnal.*]—F.J.C.

Shh, Jesus Is Talking

Be still, and know that I am God. Ps. 46:10, NKJV.

I'm so glad you've come to have a quiet time with Jesus. Cuddle up close, and listen as I tell why starting your day with Jesus is so important.

I'm sure you know that Jesus made all the trees and flowers. Can you make trees and flowers? No, of course not. But Jesus can. He is very powerful. All He has to do is think something in His mind and say He wants it to be, and it is so! Isn't it great that we can really get to know someone as wonderful as Jesus?

Quiet times with Jesus help us know Him better. Jesus likes to visit with you. You can't see Him sitting in your room, talking to you, but if you are very still, you might hear a little thought in your head that whispers *I love you very much.*

The Bible says that Jesus speaks to us in a quiet voice. You know how noisy your house can get? There is lots of noise when the baby is crying, the TV is on, the dishwasher is running, and the phone is ringing. It's difficult to hear someone whisper in all that noise.

When everything is quiet and you are cuddled up close, then you can hear Jesus' quiet thoughts. You might hear Jesus whisper a different thought in your mind as you listen to the stories in this book. I know that as you spend quiet times with Jesus, you will get to know Him better and better. —K.N.

Jesus Can Do Anything

Ah, Lord God! Behold, You have made the heavens and the earth by Your great power. . . . There is nothing too hard for You. Jer. 32:17, NKJV.

You might be learning to tie your shoe. Is it hard to learn? I bet it is. Learning new things is hard for most of us.

Or you might be learning to write your name. That's very hard to learn also. You probably practice a lot to make it look just right.

Do you think you could build a real space rocket? No, that would be too hard for you. Could you make a tall mountain covered with trees, grass, rivers, and lakes? Of course not! That would be impossible.

Would you like to know something fantastic about Jesus? OK, listen carefully. Jesus can do *anything*! Nothing is too hard for Him. Nothing is impossible for Him.

I don't know, but I could guess that you might need a little of His help for something that seems hard for you.

Is it hard to obey sometimes? Jesus can help you, because nothing is too hard for Him.

Do you need to find something that you lost? Jesus can help you. Nothing is too hard for Him.

Do you need help to be kind and share with your sister or brother? Jesus can help you. Nothing is too hard for Him.

Jesus especially loves to answer the prayers for help from little children. You can ask Him to help you with anything. Nothing is too hard for Him.

See, I told you that was fantastic! You might want to listen to the verse for today again. —K.N.

Jesus' Surprise

In my Father's house are many [rooms]. . . . I go to prepare a place for you. John 14:2, NKJV.

Have you ever colored a picture for your mom and dad? Maybe you went to your room and colored it so that it would be a surprise. Do you remember how excited you felt? You could hardly wait to give it to them!

Jesus is getting a surprise ready for *you.* He's very excited about it, and He can hardly wait to give it to you. He's making a special room just for you in heaven. Your room won't be like anyone else's, because you aren't like anyone else.

Jesus can hardly wait to come get you and take you to live forever with Him. He wants all your family to come too.

No one loves you more than Jesus. No one has a better plan for you than Jesus. His plan is for you and your family and everyone who loves Him with all their heart to live forever with Him.

Jesus has promised to come back to earth and take you and your family to heaven. Would you like to tell Jesus that you want to go home with Him?

Worship Activities

• Have your child describe his or her imagining of the room in heaven that Jesus is preparing.

• Help your child memorize John 14:1-3.

• Have everyone draw a picture of heaven. [Sparkle glue, glitter, puffy paints, etc., will help make this picture special.]—K.N.

Being Kind to Jesus

And the King will answer, . . . "As you did it to one of the least of these My brethren, you did it to Me." Matt. 25:40, NKJV.

Jesus told lots of stories when He was here on earth. One day He told a story about how important it is to be kind and to do nice things to others, especially if they really need it.

Jesus said that when we are nice to others, it is just as if we are being nice to Him. If we are mean or selfish to others, it is just like being mean to Jesus.

I thought you might want to know about this story that Jesus told. You probably have a brother or sister or friends you play with. Did you know that when you are kind and share your toys with them that you are also being nice to Jesus?

I'm quite sure that if Jesus were in this room, you would share your best toy with Him. Or you would be happy to let Him go first. And if He were hurt, you would quickly help Him.

You may know someone who doesn't have very many toys or books. You can share some of your toys or books with that person. If you do, you will be sharing with Jesus too!

Do you know what makes me sad? When you are unkind or selfish to your brother or sister or friends, I feel sad. And Jesus feels bad too, because it is as if you are unkind or selfish to Him.

Now that you know about this story Jesus told and what it means, I'm sure you will remember to treat all people with love and kindness. —K.N.

Jesus Obeyed When He Was Little

※ *Children, obey your parents in all things, for this is well pleasing to the Lord. Col. 3:20, NKJV.*

Do you ever wonder what Jesus did when He was a little boy? I thought you might like to know about one of the things the Bible tells us Jesus did when He was little.

The Bible tells us that Jesus obeyed His parents (Luke 2:11). That tells us a lot about Jesus.

Would you imagine with me for a few minutes? What would Jesus do if His mother asked Him to put away His toys? Would He whine and complain? Would He just keep on playing? Or would He quickly put away His toys? Yes! You're right. Jesus would quickly obey.

Imagine again. Jesus loved all the beautiful things in nature. He loved to play outdoors. What do you think Jesus would do if He was playing outside and His dad called for Him? Would He pretend not to hear? Would He say, "I'll be there in a little bit"? Or would He come right away to see what His dad needed? Yes! You're right again. Jesus would obey quickly.

Do you want to be like Jesus? He wants you to be. But He knows how hard it is for little boys and girls to obey quickly. So He has made a way to help you obey your parents.

Because Jesus was always obedient, He is able to help you obey. Do you need help to obey? Yes, you do. Even your mommy and daddy need help to obey. Do you want Jesus to help you? He will. Jesus loves to help children remember to obey. Do you believe that He will help you? Then all you must do is ask for His help.

Anytime you need Jesus' help to obey, just ask Him. He will be happy to help you. —K.N.

Growing Like Jesus

And the Child grew and became strong, . . . filled with wisdom.
Luke 2:40, NKJV.

Y ou are growing. Every day you are getting bigger and bigger. Every day you learn new things. Most of the time growing is fun. Because you are bigger than you used to be, you can dress yourself now. That's fun. But sometimes growing hurts. Because your feet are growing and you're not very good at running yet, sometimes you fall down, and that hurts!

Jesus knows about growing. He was little too. The Bible says that Jesus "grew and became strong, . . . filled with wisdom."

Do you know what wisdom is? Wisdom is knowing the difference between right and wrong, and then doing what is right. When you share your toys, you are being wise. When you let someone else go first, you are being wise. When you ask questions and then listen carefully to the answer, you are being wise.

Wisdom is also eating the foods that are best for you, obeying your parents, and spending quiet times with Jesus.

You can grow just like Jesus did. You can grow with wisdom. When you grow with wisdom, everyone has more fun. You may still fall down and hurt yourself, but you will know that it is part of growing. After a hug and a kiss you can go out to play some more.

Have fun today as you grow strong with wisdom. —K.N.

Zacchaeus Meets Jesus

Zacchaeus, make haste and come down, for today I must stay at your house. Luke 19:5, NKJV.

I love the stories about Jesus. He was so kind and gentle. Do you remember the story of Zacchaeus? Zacchaeus did some very bad things. He lied. He cheated. He took money that did not really belong to him. I don't think you've done all those bad things.

Even though Zacchaeus did many bad things, Jesus still loved him and wanted to be friends with him. Zacchaeus had heard how kind and gentle Jesus was. Zacchaeus began to be sorry for all the bad things he had done. He really wanted to meet Jesus and get to know Him better too.

The day that Jesus came to Zacchaeus' town, Zacchaeus knew he could finally see Jesus. But Zacchaeus was short, too short to see over the heads and shoulders of everyone else. Zacchaeus didn't push or shove or get angry. Instead he became creative and found a tree to climb.

Aren't you glad that Jesus stopped right under that tree and looked up to talk with Zacchaeus? I sure am.

When you really want to get to know Jesus better, He will always come to meet you. No matter what bad things you may have done, Jesus still loves you and wants to spend time with you.

You can't see Jesus now when you come to have a quiet time with Him. But you can know He's here because of the love and the peace and the happiness you feel.

I'm quite sure that Zacchaeus was very happy to meet with Jesus. I'm glad you came to spend quiet time with Jesus too. And so is Jesus. —K.N.

You Are Special

I will praise You, for I am . . . wonderfully made. Ps. 139:14, NKJV.

Look at the inside of your hands. Do you see the small lines that go across your hand? Now look at the ends of your fingers. You see even smaller lines that curve over the tops of your fingers.

The lines in your hands and fingers are very special. No one in the world has lines just like yours. Your brother's or sister's or friends' lines aren't just like yours. Your lines are even different from your mom's and dad's.

Now every time you look at your hands and fingers, you will know that you are very special. Jesus made you that way. He made your smile and eyes special. He made your thinking and feeling special. No one else thinks or feels just like you.

You are the only one in the world who is just like you.

Have you noticed other children who are different from you? They are supposed to be! Their fingerprints, smile, eyes, thinking, and feeling are special to them.

I think it is wonderful how Jesus makes us each special and then loves us because we are each so special.

When we notice the differences in each other, we can see how creative Jesus is. Just think. He made all the different animals and flowers. He made all the stars and has a name for each one (Ps. 147:4). Because Jesus made you special, He will never forget you. Isn't Jesus wonderful?

Worship Activity

● Make a fingerprint poster with your child's picture, fingerprints, and today's verse. —K.N.

213

Open the Door

Behold, I stand at the door and knock. If anyone . . . opens the door, I will come in . . . and dine with him. Rev. 3:20, NKJV.

Do you know how to imagine? Of course you do. Imagine that you are in your most favorite room in your house. Is it the living room? the kitchen? or your bedroom? Imagine yourself doing something fun in that room. Is anyone with you? You can tell whoever is reading to you all about it if you want.

Now imagine looking out the window of that room and seeing Jesus walking toward your house. What would you do? What does Jesus look like to you? Listen for the knock. Yes, that's Jesus knocking on your door. Will you answer the door? Or will your parents?

Imagine that Jesus is now inside your house. Where would He sit? Where are you in that room? What does His face look like?

Now imagine that Jesus asks to stay for dinner. Do you want to sit next to Him? What do you think you would talk to Jesus about? I know He'd be happy to listen. He might even tickle you and play cars or dolls with you while you wait for dinner.

Your mind and feeling place are like a house with a door. Jesus wants to come live in your thinking place. He wants you to know that He will be with you all the time and everywhere you go. Can you imagine Him knocking at the door to your thinking and feeling place? If you open that door or say "Yes, Jesus, come in," He will do just that. You can have His love inside of you. His love will help you share when you play and be cheerful when you obey. —K.N.

Two Fathers

Show us the Father. . . . Jesus said, . . . "He who has seen Me has seen the Father." John 14:8, 9, NKJV.

If I sent you a picture of me, you would say, "Oh, that's what Mrs. Nicola looks like." But you really wouldn't know me.

But if every day I sent you letters telling about what I like to eat and how I like to dress and what I like to do, you would get to know me a little bit better.

Now, if I sent you my daughter, who acts a lot like I do and thinks a lot like I do, you would get to know me even better.

When Jesus came to live here, He came to show us what God the Father is really like.

First Jesus *told* us that His Father, God, is also our Father. That means you have two fathers. One probably lives in your house, plays with you, helps you, and tucks you into bed at night. But you also have a heavenly Father, who always watches over you and loves you even more than your daddy.

Second, Jesus *showed* us how kind and gentle the Father is. Jesus was kind and gentle. Jesus loved to do nice things for others. Jesus understood how other people felt. Jesus acted just like His heavenly Father would act.

When Jesus died for your sins and mine, He really showed us how much our Father in heaven loves us. When we believe that Jesus forgives our sins, that makes our heavenly Father very happy. When we believe that Jesus gives us eternal life, that makes our heavenly Father very happy. When we thank Him for Jesus, that makes our heavenly Father very happy.

Our heavenly Father has given us the beautiful things of nature to *teach* us about Him. He gave us the Bible to *tell* us about Him. When you spend quiet times with Jesus, you are also getting to know God the Father better. Our heavenly Father is wonderful! —K.N.

Diamonds in the Weeds

Your paths drip with abundance. They drop on the pastures of the wilderness, and the little hills rejoice on every side. Ps. 65:11, 12, NKJV.

The big storm was over. The sky was blue again. The grass looked extra green. Mom and Joanna hurried to get their coats and boots on. They were going for a walk.

As they walked up the road, Joanna splashed in every mud puddle, giggling all the way. She was so happy to be outside with Mother! As they were walking home they saw something that caught their attention.

When Mother and Joanna got closer to them, they discovered tiny lupine plants.

"Look," Mother said, and pointed as they bent over to take a closer look. "The lupine leaves each have a tiny droplet of rain in the center. Each droplet is shining like a beautiful diamond. A diamond is a crystal clear rock," Mother explained.

Mother and Joanna looked at all the different sizes of droplets in each cluster of leaves. The sun made them look beautiful!

"You know, sweetie," said Mother, "I'm so glad God made these tiny water diamonds in the weeds for us to enjoy this morning."

Joanna nodded and smiled as she reached out her hand to pick a little stem. As soon as she did, the water droplet slipped down through the leaf cluster and onto her fingers.

"Oh!" laughed Joanna, "it's all gone! Water diamonds sure don't last long."

Worship Activities

- Have your child draw a picture of the story.
- Repeat the scripture. Thank Jesus for some of the "tiny" blessings in your lives. —K.N.

Here, Birdie

☀ *Look at the birds of the air. . . . Are you not of more value than they? Matt. 6:26, NKJV.*

S eth, Mother, and Elizabeth were especially happy to be at the park. It was wintertime, but the sun was out and the air felt warm. The birds were happy in the sunshine too. Many birds were on the grass, looking for worms.

Seth really wanted to hold a bird. They looked so easy to catch down there on the ground. Very, very slowly and quietly, Seth walked toward a bird. He held out his hand and softly said, "Here, birdie; here, birdie." Just about the time Seth got close enough to touch the bird, it flew away. Seth laughed and laughed. Then he very quietly tried to catch another one. But each time the bird would fly away.

That night as Mommy was putting Seth to bed, they talked about heaven. Mommy talked about all the animals Seth could play with in heaven.

"I want a real little bird to sit on my shoulder," Seth said. "I can't wait to see Jesus and all the birds He has made for me," he added.

"Seth," said Mommy, "I'm very glad that Jesus has all kinds of beautiful birds just waiting for you in heaven. But I'm extra glad that *you* want to live in heaven. And that makes Jesus extra, extra glad."

Thought Questions

• What kind of bird would you like to hold in heaven?

• Why do you think Jesus is extra, extra glad to know you want to live with Him in heaven?—K.N.

Busy Days

Happy are the people whose God is the Lord! Ps. 144:15, NKJV.

Every once in a while we all have a busy day. Sometimes a whole day can be filled with errands. That's how Gerrad's and Mother's day was.

First they went to the post office. Then to the feed store. After that they went to the bank. Then to the park for a picnic lunch. After lunch they went to the library. Finally they went to the market.

"It's hard to ride in the car seat for a long time, Mommy," Gerrad said as they drove home.

"I'm sure it is," Mother answered.

In a few minutes Gerrad was sound asleep. "Are we home?" Gerrad asked sleepily when the car stopped in the driveway.

Mommy opened Gerrad's door, unbuckled his car seat belt, and lifted him into her arms. It felt good to lay his head on her shoulder.

From Mommy's shoulder, Gerrad looked up and saw the evening star. He pointed to it.

"Mommy, look! The evening star."

Mommy and Gerrad stood there for a long time, looking at the star. Their busy day was over. Mommy hugged Gerrad and gave him a kiss.

Gerrad was thinking, *Being with Jesus is like this happy way I feel when I'm in Mommy's arms and looking at the evening star.*

Worship Activity

● Talk about different experiences you have had with your child and how he or she felt. How would your child feel if he or she were with Jesus?—K.N.

Dawdling Renée

☀ *In the day of my trouble I sought the Lord. Ps. 77:2, NKJV.*

Hurry and get ready for bed," Mother urged as she and Renée walked in the door after kids' choir.

By the time Mother got upstairs, Renée was only half undressed.

Once more Mother asked Renée to get her clothes off and jammies on. Then get her teeth brushed. But Renée kept on dawdling.

Tonight, because Renée took so very long to obey and get ready for bed, Mother decided that they would have to skip the usual bedtime story.

Renée didn't like that idea, and began to sob and wail. "I feel like doing something I don't want to do!" she cried.

"Can you tell me what you feel like doing?" Mother asked.

"I feel like kicking and screaming."

"Do you think Jesus wants you to kick and scream?" asked Mother.

"No," sobbed Renée.

"How about praying and asking Jesus to take away the feeling to kick and scream?" suggested Mother.

Together Mother and Renée prayed. "Dear Jesus, thank You that I can have feelings. Thank You that You helped me tell them to my mother. Thank You that I can tell them to You too. I don't really like these feelings, though, to kick and scream. Please take them away. Please give me Your feeling of peace. I love You. Amen."

And Jesus did just that.

Questions

● Have you ever felt like Renée? Can you tell me about it?

● Did you know Jesus can help you with your feelings?—K.N.

Melony's Pets

✷A *good man is concerned for the welfare of his animals.* Prov. 12:10, TLB.

Melony is a little girl, probably about as big as you are. Melony loves animals. She likes puppies, kittens, cats, dogs, ponies, geese, and rabbits, and she even has a pet rat.

Melony has learned to treat her pets gently. She calls to them in a nice voice. She pats them tenderly. When she holds them, she does not squeeze them tightly. She likes to help feed all the pets, and she makes sure they all have enough water.

Pets are special gifts from Jesus. Jesus made pets for us to care for and enjoy. When Melony is kind and gentle to her pets, she is taking good care of Jesus' gifts to her.

Animals cannot talk to us and tell us when they are hungry or thirsty. So we must give them the food and water, exercise, and love that they need every day. Melony is happy to take care of Jesus' animals.

Someday, when Jesus makes a brand-new heaven and a brand-new earth, all the animals can be our pets. Then children like you and Melony will have a wonderful time caring for and enjoying all Jesus' animals.

Questions

• If you could have any kind of pet, what kind would you choose? Why?

• Why do pets need people?

• How can you be kind to your pet today—if you have one?—K.N.

Jesus Is Coming Again

Jesus has gone away to heaven, and some day, just as he went, he will return! Acts 1:11, TLB.

The music from Andrew's favorite tape filled the room. Andrew and his little sister played happily together.

All of a sudden Andrew got up from his play, raised his hands to his mouth to hold an imaginary trumpet, and began to march around the room. Soon Little Sister and Mother joined him. The song "Lift Up the Trumpet" was playing. Andrew liked trumpets. But he liked the thought of Jesus' coming again even better.

Andrew, Mother, and Little Sister marched and sang until the song was over. Then, out of breath, they all collapsed onto the couch, where they laughed and cuddled.

Singing about Jesus' coming again made them all think about heaven.

"What do you want to do when we go home to heaven?" asked Mother.

"I want to hold a bird," Andrew answered, "and I want to listen to Jesus tell me stories—and see my Bible friends."

"Yes, heaven will be wonderful. I can hardly wait until Jesus comes," said Mother.

Worship Activity

• Together sing your child's favorite song about heaven or Jesus' second coming.

   Questions

• What do you want to do special with Jesus when you go home to heaven?

• Tell me what you think heaven looks like. —K.N.

God's Good Seeds

[The kingdom of God] is like a tiny mustard seed planted in a garden; soon it grows into a tall bush. Luke 13:19, TLB.

Reneé was Mother's little helper. She had finally grown big enough to help Mother plant flower seeds. Mother and Reneé made a flower box just for Reneé's seeds. Together they mixed the dirt with the fertilizer.

The seed packets lay on the ground. The pictures of the flowers looked so pretty.

"I like planting flowers with you, Mother," Reneé said.

"I'm glad you could help me this year, now that you are bigger," Mother answered.

The flower box was ready for the seeds. Reneé reached for the seed packet. She tore it open. "Oh, Mommy, they are all dead," she sighed.

"Yes, darling," Mother replied, "seeds look dead. But when we plant them in the dirt, God sends the sunshine and the water to make them grow. Then they will look like the pretty flowers in the picture. It's a miracle!

"And did you know that God wants to plant His seeds of love, kindness, joy, peace, and patience in our thinking place?"

Reneé shook her head no.

"God says that His good seeds grow beautiful thoughts and feelings in our lives. That's a miracle too!"

Question

● What kind of good seed do you want Jesus to plant in your thinking place?—K.N.

Lost on the Mountain

Hear my prayer, O Lord. . . . In the day of my trouble . . . answer me speedily. Ps. 102:1, 2, NKJV.

Alan looked all around him. Nothing looked familiar. Joanna couldn't tell which way to go either.

Alan and Joanna were neighbors. They always had a wonderful time making trails and forts in the trees and bushes near Joanna's home in the country. They lived at the top of a small mountain that was thick with trees and bushes.

But today Alan and Joanna had wandered farther than they had planned, and now they were lost. They tried walking in one direction and then another.

Joanna and Alan were beginning to get frightened. Then Joanna said, "Let's pray."

Although Alan wasn't used to praying, he agreed.

"Dear Jesus," Joanna prayed, "please help us find our way home. Amen."

Then Joanna and Alan began to call loudly. "M-o-t-h-e-r!"

Although Mother was in the house with the windows and doors closed, she heard a faint cry for help. Running outside, Mother called back, "J-o-a-n-n-a! Follow the sound of my voice."

In just a few seconds Alan and Joanna walked out of the trees and bushes and were once again in the backyard. They were safe, and they were happy to be home.

Questions

- How would you feel if you were lost?
- How long did Jesus take to answer Joanna's prayer?
- Will He answer your prayers for help too?—K.N.